*...where the Spirit of the Lord is,
there is freedom.*

2 Corinthians 3:17

Melchizedek Frequencies Volume 1
Activating Your Priesthood by Harmonizing Your Being
Adonijah O. Ogbonnaya, Ph.D.

Publications Copyright © 2024, literature arm of AACTEV8 International
(Apostolic Activation Network) Aactev8 International
1020 Victoria Ave.
Venice, CA 90291
www.aactev8.com

Published by Seraph Creative

Print ISBN: 978-1-964959-12-2
eBook ISBN: 978-1-964959-13-9
Library of Congress data

The English Standard Version (ESV) is used for all Scripture references unless
otherwise noted.

New King James Version (NKJV): Scripture taken from the New King James
Version®. Copyright ©1982 by Tomas Nelson. Used by permission. All
rights reserved.

Italics in Scripture are added by the author.
Editor: Kathy Strecker

Cover art: Typesetting, Illustration & Layout by Feline Graphics
www.felinegraphics.com

Melchizedek Frequencies

Volume One

Activating Your Priesthood
By Harmonizing Your Being

Dr. Adonijah Ogbonnaya Ph.D.

ACKNOWLEDGEMENTS

Although it is possible to write a book like this one by oneself, it is not necessarily advisable or wise. What we do is for the benefit of humankind and involves the energy of humanity to bring it to fruition. If it were not for the loving input and care of the many people around me, this book would not exist—at least not at this time. It is their love, care, and dedication that has made this work possible while giving me freedom to pursue other areas of research and teaching without being stuck. All the ideas in this book, along with their success or failure to please the reader, are mine. However, I would be remiss if I did not express my gratitude for the work done by many others to bring it to publication.

I thank my publisher, Chris Blackeby, and his team, Linda Lurie and Leigh Brett. I am grateful to Kathy Strecker who edited the book, Ronald Montijn who transcribed and did

some editing of the manuscript, and John Eichelberger who read and offered input on the second draft.

I am especially grateful for my hard-working staff, Edward Johnson and Monique Tyson, who coordinate my publications and do so much to help keep them on track.

I thank the Melchizedek Church of Nashville, Pastor Donald Crossland, and all the staff who gave me the opportunity to teach this material to the church before I wrote the book. Thanks to all my students who study with me. Our interactions allow me to seek deeper places of relationship and cultivate more openness to new depths of revelatory knowledge from the Word.

My deepest thanks and gratitude are for the Word Made Flesh, Yeshua, our Lord and Master, who deserves all glory and honor. AMEN!

Adonijah Ogbonnaya
Lake Elsinore, CA
2024

Contents

INTRODUCTION

The name Melchizedek, which was introduced in the story of our father Abraham, has elicited many interpretations in Western religious literature. In this brief book, I have endeavored to add my voice from a different perspective to give the reader a view into Melchizedek that he/she may never have been given before. To the symphony of earnest interpreters of the revelation of Melchizedek, I say that my alchemical crucible of revelatory engagement with the Spirit is sure to contribute to understanding this mysterious being called Melchizedek.

From this desire and perspective, I have limited the scope of this book and focused on the frequencies of life that Melchizedek represents for those who will engage in his mystery.

This book is the first of a three-volume work on Melchizedek. The first volume deals with what I call *Melchizedek Frequencies*. The second volume deals with *Melchizedek Consciousness*, and the third volume deals with Melchizedek Rays.

When speaking of Melchizedek, one should naturally think of the Messiah, our father Abraham, King David, and of course, the Aaronic Priesthood that represented an outflow of the principle of his being. Therefore, I present first the stories from the ancient world, especially the Bible, that illustrate the importance of Melchizedek. Then I lay the framework for understanding the priesthood of Melchizedek.

In this volume, I navigate the meaning, scope, and hidden mysteries of the Melchizedek frequencies. The idea of frequencies is to point to the spiritual vibrational impact of certain dimensions of this priesthood in terms of human relationships with God, with one another, and with the created worlds. The Melchizedek frequency is the mystical structuring of priestly activities that unlocks the hidden tones of heaven in the normal, daily priestly mode of being in the world. This book is meant to map and bring clarity to systems that are intrinsically "Melchizedek" in nature and to move the reader to look at their divine/human responsibility in new ways. The true work of the Melchizedek Priesthood has its beginning in his first meeting with Abraham, which demonstrates the rectification and perfecting of creation through the divine/human relationship.

Human activities, when done in conjunction with Melchizedek principles, emit specific transformational frequencies both for us and the world. In this book, you will read about some of these activities, their frequencies, and their potential transformational impact on the world at large, your personal life, and that of your family and friends. What is the Melchizedek frequency of sacrifice and how does it impact the way the believer lives life? What is the relationship between the principles of the Melchizedek Priesthood and our calling to the construct of divine sonship? What do Melchizedek frequencies say about our impact in creation?

The human will, in my opinion, emits a particular kind of frequency that influences and directs how the world responds to us and how we also respond to it. What does it look like to be attuned to the Melchizedek frequency and how does it impact our divine destiny in the current world and maybe even in the world to come? All the aspects of the Melchizedek life call us to emit frequencies and vibrations that impact, transmute, and transform our world. Kingship, sonship, rest, respect and honor, scientific knowledge—almost all human activities done for Divine/human goals can be tuned to a Melchizedek frequency that can bring rectification to the world.

The grand idea is that the Word, which became flesh in the man Yeshua Ha Mashiach, is God being initiated into the priesthood after the Order of Melchizedek. This initiation makes it possible to insert the God frequency into the human *being* and the human *acting*. Consequently, my actions (the acts of any believer) in the Melchizedek Priesthood, obtained before God through Yeshua Ha Mashiach (Jesus the Christ), emit the same frequency that Jesus the Christ emitted through His initiation into His role as the High Priest.

These are just a few points we will explore in this Melchizedek phenomenon. As you read, I encourage you to live out the Melchizedek life and emit these frequencies in your own divine being and acting.

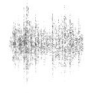

INTRODUCTION

Chapter 1

THE FREQUENCY
OF SACRIFICE

Hebrews 1-8 is all about Melchizedek. I think it is set up to prove that Jesus Christ is inserted into the Melchizedek order. For a long time, we were taught that Melchizedek is Jesus, but He is not. There are two orders of priesthood recognized by God: the Aaronic Priesthood, of which I am one by blood, and the Melchizedek Priesthood.

There is a group of people living in South Africa called the Lemba Tribe.[1] As far as we know, they are the largest people group on earth that is allowed to sacrifice in the temple, if one were to be built. They have a very dark skin color and are direct descendants of Aaron. Now what does that mean? In the context of Hebrews 1-8, one family line mentions Jesus Christ. All eight chapters are about Melchizedek, but they also show that Jesus Christ was initiated into the order of Melchizedek. God decreed that Jesus should be inserted there, but God Himself was not the one who put him into the order of Melchizedek. God spoke, but in order to be a priest, you must first participate in the life of the people for whom you are going to serve as a priest.

You cannot be an outsider and still be a priest. Even as God, Jesus was not automatically qualified to be initiated into the order of Melchizedek. Jesus could not become the High Priest unless He first became a man. If Jesus was only God, He could be a priest in heaven only, not for humanity. To be a priest for any people or family, you must first participate in the bloodline of the people. Jesus could not have been a High Priest if He had not become a man.

Jesus Christ is the eternal Son of God, but Jesus is not a High Priest in the Godhead. Jesus' nature is exactly the same as that of the Father and the Holy Spirit. This means that Jesus always existed from the very moment God was God. The second person of the Godhead has always been in the Godhead and is co-equal with the Father and the Holy Spirit. This results in a *perichoretic* movement. "Perichoresis"[2] is a great Christian word that you should learn. It refers to the interpenetration of beings, meaning that the complete

---

1 https://en.wikipedia.org/wiki/Lemba_people

2 Perichoresis from Greek: περιχώρησις perikhōrēsis, «rotation» is a term referring to the relationship of the three persons of the triune God (Father, Son, and Holy Spirit) to one another. https://en.wikipedia.org/wiki/Perichoresis

being of God is in Him. Every person of the Godhead fully contains the other two completely within themselves.

When the second person of the Godhead was still in heaven, His name was not Jesus. He was simply God. Christianity believes in one God *in* three persons, not one God *and* three persons. This means that when you see one person of the Godhead, you have seen the rest. If you see the Father, you have also seen the Holy Spirit and the Son. That is why Scripture says,

> **"For in Him dwells all the fullness of the Godhead bodily."[3]**

Everywhere one goes, the rest of the Godhead goes, too.

If you have the Holy Spirit right now, then the Father and the Son operate within the Spirit while the Spirit does the frontal work. The person we are talking about is the very God of the very God, the very light of the very light. We are not talking about a god that appeared only recently on Earth. Jesus did not become God when He became a human being. Jesus Christ was not a human being who was later made into God. Jesus was God by His very essence and became a human being.

When we talk about Melchizedek, I often hear people say many things. This Son in God, who is God, and wherever He goes, the other two are with Him. In creation, the Father was the foremost being and used the Spirit and the Word to create the world. This means that the Father was in the forefront, and the other two were instrumental. However, one of the things we have not done effectively is understand that the Spirit is in the forefront—one of the things we are going to unwrap in this book.

---

3   Colossians 2:9

Jesus himself said that He is going in the background and the Spirit will take over. As Pentecostals, we seem to have misunderstood this, as we still act as if the Spirit is not present. However, Jesus said that if He does not go, the Spirit will not come. Jesus said that He was leaving us with the Spirit; meaning that in our age, the Spirit is in the forefront. Please understand me—Jesus Christ is still Lord, but you are in the Age of the Holy Spirit.

In the redemptive and preservative principles of creation, the Son took the forefront, but the Holy Spirit and the Father were still present in redemption. If the Father and the Spirit were not present in Christ, redemption would have been incomplete. We are dealing with someone who is fully God and became fully human. He was not partially human, but fully human.

Before creation, God was completely God. With the intent of creation, the second person of the Godhead had to step into prominence. The Bible says,

"Jesus Christ is the Lamb of God who was slain before the foundation of the world."[4]

I know many people say, "from the foundation," but in this case, it is not "from." The Greek word "apo"[5] can mean "from," but it can also mean "before." This means that Jesus Christ is not the foundation of the world. So then, who is the foundation of the world? You are. The Bible says that the righteous are the foundation of the world. Not God. Not Jesus. Not the Holy Spirit. The Bible clearly says that you are

---

4   Revelation 13:8

5   Strong's G 575 ἀπό hereafter, ago, at, because of, before. A primary particle; "off," i.e. Away (from something near), in various senses (of place, time, or relation; literal or figurative) -- (X here-)after, ago, at, because of, before, by (the space of), for(-th), from, in, (out) of, off, (up-)on(-ce), since, with. In composition (as a prefix) it usually denotes separation, departure, cessation, completion, reversal.

the foundation of the world.[6] The Hebrew uses two words: the word for *foundation* is "Yesod" and the word for *world* is "Olam."[7]

Again, Jesus is not the foundation of the world; He is that which is before the foundation of the world. He is what theologians call the ground of being. There cannot be a foundation without the ground. Jesus is the ground, and we are the foundation. But for Jesus Christ to be the fabric upon which the foundation is laid, He had to die. This is not a death like you and I experience, but His life still had to be given. There was no death before creation,[8] only the possibility of a change of substance.

God became a Lamb, which means there was a change of substance. But the substance of His being had to be shed so He could become the ground upon which the righteous could become the foundation. That is why wisdom was rejoicing in you before you were made. The person you are calling God took on a form that God had never taken before. Since Jesus took that form, and the righteous are the foundation of the world, something had to happen. God has always had in His mind that we would become part of the Godhead. You and I will be part of the Godhead. If not, why did He take a human body into the Godhead? There is a human body sitting in heaven right now. Jesus did not just go to heaven; He is sitting in the center of God. There is a body in the midst of the triune God. He was slain before the foundation of the world,[9] and *you* are the foundation of worlds. Wisdom, which is an outgrowth of the intentionality of Divinity,

---

6   Proverbs 10:25
7   יְסוֹד Yesod foundation, base) Strong's H 3247 and עוֹלָם Olam (long duration, antiquity, futurity, world) Strong's 5769
8   Romans 5:12
9   Revelations 13:8

was looking and said, "Those are the people in whom I am rejoicing!" Incredible!

Yet before that can happen, that Lamb, that substance which God became in a realm where there was no death, had to be slain. And since there was no death before creation, if it were slain, the result can only be life, not death.

So who then must slay the Lamb? It cannot be God, because you cannot show me one place in Scripture where it says that the Father killed Jesus. You may have heard people say, "the Father slew His only Son," but the Bible does not actually say that. In fact, the Bible teaches against it.[10] This is why, when Abraham took Isaac up, God did not let him kill Isaac.

It is illegal, both in Divinity and in creation, for a father to slay his own child, so much so that God made a law in Israel that they must not offer up their own children as a sacrifice.[11] In other words, they must not slay their own children. It is an eternal law that a father is not supposed to kill his own child.

But think about it. Who is going to kill this Lamb, this God who has taken on a different substance? It must be a priest. However, you cannot be the priest of an order of which you are not a part. Jesus did not become an Israelite. He became a human being. Let me try to clarify. He was a Jew, but He did not become Jewish. The Bible never said that Jesus became Jewish, not once. The Bible never said that He became an Israelite. Instead, the Bible says that the Lord Jesus Christ became "Anthropos" or human He became "Adam."[12]

---

10 Leviticus 20:2-5
11 Leviticus 18:21
12 Philippians 2:6-8

Who killed Jesus on Calvary? Human beings and priests! Who slew Jesus before the foundation of the world? A priest! And the only priest that God had already projected was a human being. So, Melchizedek is the summative principle of the human beings who are the priests of God.

That means that you and I slew Jesus. You and I slew the Lamb before the foundation of the world. If you recall what happened on Calvary, human beings slew the Lord Jesus Christ. You cannot have it different in the beginning. There must be consistency between the two events, and they must have an arc.

What is this arc? Melchizedek represents the summative principle of the entire body of humanity, even before the world was created. This means that God reached into the future, bringing you and me into existence to slay the Lamb before the foundation of the world. The Bible says that Melchizedek has no father or mother, and does not have a beginning or an end.[13] Who else on earth is like that? Only those who are born from above. If you are born from heaven, then you are born from God.

This is a simple teaching that I have repeated many times, but it is good to remind Christians. If you are born of God, and we know that what is born of the Spirit *is* Spirit, then you have the very nature of God.[14] You cannot be anything other than what gives birth to you. If I am born of God, then I am god, or at least I have the nature of God.

Because God gave birth to me, I have a different nature. If you do not believe that, then remove it from Scripture. The Lord Jesus Christ says,

13 Hebrews 7:3
14 1 John 5:1-4

"That which is born of the flesh is flesh, and that which is born of the Spirit is spirit."[15]

This means that if you are born from heaven and of the Spirit, you *are* Spirit. You are not becoming Spirit. If God gave birth to you, then His nature is in you. We do not like saying this because it sounds arrogant like we are saying we are gods. But we are not the big God. We are just baby gods. A baby god has the same nature as the big God, but does not know how to use his power yet, right? Do you have something that your baby does not have, apart from material things? We make a big mistake by thinking that there is something lacking in us. God is training us to be like Him, to act like Him. How would He do that if the godlike nature was not already in us?

Why is it difficult for some believers to accept? Because we refuse to accept the fact that everything in Him is already in us. The issue is that we are being trained to be able to use it. It would be arrogant to think we now have it and can use it effectively, because look at all the messes we make. We are acting like children. We have hands just like God, but we pick things up and wobble and fall, and things break. That does not mean our parts are different; it just means they are not trained. It does not mean our mind is less godlike, because we have the mind of Christ. It just means we do not know how to use it yet. Once we acknowledge that we have access to all of this, we must train ourselves to use it. Humility will force us to begin to practice and learn, instead of trying to teach other people.

Do you understand now? You are completely and absolutely divine. Angels see you as God unless you are not considered His child. Can you explain why this is a problem for some of you? I know some religious beliefs may be getting in the way,

15 John 3:6

but God gave birth to you. I did not say it; the Master did. But if you do not accept this simple truth and the things that are of this world, how can you believe me when I tell you all the things I want to share?

What I just told you is an earthly thing. Jesus himself said that being born from heaven is an earthly term. He told Nicodemus,

> **"If I have told you earthly things and you do not believe, how can you believe if I tell you heavenly things?"[16]**

Jesus was saying that being born from above is an earthly thing because it is directed towards the earth. If you do not believe that, how can you believe anything else? Being born from above is part of what Paul is discussing in the book of Hebrews when he talks about elementary things.[17] The writers of Hebrews even said the resurrection is part of the doctrine of first principles; it is a foundational Christian teaching. In chapter six, the author of Hebrews even says that everything you and I are struggling with is elementary.

Elementary things include repentance, faith, baptism, forgiveness of sin, the resurrection of the dead, and the final judgment. These are things that happen on earth, not in heaven. So when you begin to manifest your divine nature, you will have moved beyond that. The resurrection becomes irrelevant once you attain the nature of God and no longer need to die. If God were to transmute you right now and give you an eternal body, you would not need resurrection. Resurrection is only necessary on earth, not in heaven. The Lord Jesus Christ had to die and be resurrected in order to make it possible for us to be transmuted in an instant if we

16 John 3:12
17 Hebrews 6:1-3

align ourselves with the right frequency. This is what the Bible is teaching us.[18]

So, who slew Him? This is where Melchizedek comes in. Melchizedek represents and embodies the garment of the believers, those who stand outside of time and will be at the end of time. This means it was humanity who slayed the Lamb! How do we know that Melchizedek represents humanity? We know because Jesus was inserted into the priesthood of humanity, not the priesthood of Israel. Melchizedek represents a priesthood that is not of the Israelites.

We must look at some of the frequencies surrounding the Melchizedek Priesthood as well as the frequency of angelic relationship and understand what they mean. Who are you? Every person who becomes a believer, no matter their age, joins this priesthood. This means that by divine fiat and activity, the believer leaves this realm and participates in the slaying of the Lamb before the foundation of the world. If you were not involved in that slaying, you cannot be involved in what that being does during this age. You cannot participate in what He brings forth. This is because the Melchizedek Priesthood that was in the mind of God before the world was created *is you*, the sons of men in whom Wisdom rejoiced when the world was formed.[19] Your conversion is powerful because of this. However, we do not take the time to understand what it means to have been born from above. I never understood it either, until the Lord showed me.

I used to think that conversion was just something I was doing here until one day, while reading the Scripture, He told me that the angels of heaven rejoice over one sinner— not just a few angels, but the angels of heaven! This means that even one conversion is a cosmic event. The day you

---

18 1 Corinthians 15:52
19 Proverbs 8:31

gave your life to Christ, the whole universe readjusted itself. Listen carefully! Every time someone says "Yes" to Christ, all the angels in heaven and throughout creation stop. This is the only time the angels stop worshiping and start rejoicing, not focused on God, but focused on the person coming into the kingdom.[20]

Now, if we do not understand this foundation, what are we discussing? The thing is, you cannot be a member of the Melchizedek order if you have not been born from above. Being born from above removes you from time and places you before God. It does not mention anything about creating the heavens and the earth; it is a spiritual time warp. When you say yes to Christ and God, what happens? God suspends all laws and places you before Him. In that moment, God speaks the word to create the universe, because you must be there, making the foundational sacrifice as a priest. God provides the offering; you make the sacrifice.

Let us return to examining our position in Melchizedek. The first place to start is with the resonance of your being. The frequency of your being is fundamentally tied to Melchizedek because that is where you come from. Christ is a member of your order, which means God subjected himself to become part of our priestly order. He did not go through Levi because if He had, Jesus would have been from an order of Israel and would have subjected himself to the shadow. The Levitical Priesthood is the shadow of the Melchizedek Priesthood, which is the original template that belongs to all humanity.

By the way, this is my problem with many people on social media who talk about the tithe as though it was created by Moses. They are forgetting that the tithe is connected to the Melchizedek Principle. The tithe is a sacrifice for humanity,

not just a sacrifice for the church. It is a requirement for every nation on earth, not just for Israelites. I want to educate you about the tithe because I believe that, all too often, believers blindly follow whatever they have been taught about tithing without thinking it through.

A tithe is 10%, correct? And 10% is made up of 1 and 0, the same 1 and 0 that are the foundation of creation. This means that the tithe has probably nothing to do with what you think it is. Tithing is not a church doctrine; it is a principle of creation. When Abram gave Melchizedek a tithe, he was participating in a human principle that was established before the creation of the world. This is how Abram created a pathway for the Messiah to come through him.

It is important to note that, as believers, we often talk about foolish things because we do not truly understand the Scriptures. Why would someone go online and talk about the tithe as if it is just a Jewish thing, especially when it was done before the Abrahamic covenant was established? It was done before Moses, before Israel became a nation, and it was done by a Gentile, not a Jew. Abram, who was a Gentile, gave the tithe to all of humanity through Melchizedek. This means that he gave you the tithe as well.

This is why Abram's descendants can draw from you, because you ate from their father, Melchizedek. The mystery of this is not understood by many. The church often says that tithing is not necessary, but I say to them, tithing is not just a Jewish thing. The Jews do it and they have access. But what happens if you do not tithe? I want to know how it is working out for you and for those who are attacking this concept online. If what I am saying has any truth to it, it means that you have missed an opportunity to draw from humanity.

I asked the Lord about this and received the understanding that, as a believer, your giving is done out of grace; however, you need to understand that the tithe is also a creative principle.

The tithe was not started by Jews. How did Abram come to know that he was supposed to give a tenth? Let me help you understand this. God put the "10" principle into Abraham's family. Abraham knew the tithe was a principle for both transmuting and accessing DNA because God gave him five and gave Sarah five when He changed their names: Abram became Abraham, and Sarai became Sarah after Abram tithed to Melchizedek. God added a Hey to each of them. The gematria of Hey is five, and when you add the Hey in Abraham and the Hey in Sarah, it equals 10. God revealed these mysteries here, but not everyone understands them. People are more concerned about material things.

When you give 20 dollars, you think you have done something. However, you do not realize that if you actually knew what you were doing, you would be opening doors and accessing your Melchizedek Principle, thereby accessing humanity before the foundation of the world. You have access to humanity before they are manifested in creation.

That is why I do what I do. I am not letting anyone take the tithe away from me. I am a Jew; I know how it works. I give more than 20 percent of my income. How much do you give? If you are fighting against the tithe, how much of your income do you give? That is the problem with Christians— they are protecting what they have instead of actually doing what they are supposed to do.

This fight against the tithe is all about hoarding and protecting what you have. This is the reason Christian billionaires and millionaires often do not leave any kind of legacy for society when they die. They provide only for their

own children. On the other hand, Jews, who make up less than 6% of society, give 26% of all charity.

Why do Christians question this Principle of Melchizedek? God has embedded in humanity the capacity for sacrifice. It is a way for God to both show and tell us that we were there before the world was created. Time means nothing to God, as evidenced by Him bringing us to the point before creation and making us our own priestly order. There, He allowed us to slay the Lamb. Even in our fallen human nature, we intrinsically understand sacrifice. When it comes to concrete and material things, we do it without even thinking because we know what it is.

The first frequency is the frequency of sacrifice because without it, nothing can pass from God into this realm. When God wanted to create the world in which you are living, He needed the frequency of sacrifice. God's voice could not have passed from divinity into the realm of creation if it was not for the sacrifice of the Lamb. That sacrifice served as the amplifying principle of God's voice. His voice served as the *fractalizing principle* of His Word. When God spoke one word and billions and trillions of species came out of that word because of the sacrifice made by the Lamb. When the voice passes through the frequency of sacrifice, it creates myriads of possibilities.

Because the principle of sacrifice is so unfamiliar to modern man, we do not understand the importance of it. You were watching God when He did that. You saw Him do it. It is in your DNA. You know deep inside of you, as one being born from heaven, that the universe would not exist without the Lamb's sacrifice. It is easy to understand that without the sacrifice you cannot be saved. Additionally, you also need to understand that without sacrifice, the universe would not exist. The grain of sand would not exist. The ocean would not exist. The stars would not exist. The galaxies would not exist.

So when God speaks one word, the sacrifice amplifies it and fractalizes it.[21] The Principle of Sacrifice is the principle of harmonic integration and proportionality. This means that when God speaks, His word can form a giant angel, and the same word can form a life because life did not exist until the moment of utterance. The frequency and resonance of sacrifice can accomplish great things for you. This Sacrifice is what makes Melchizedek such an incredible being. God's plan was for Melchizedek to appear whenever the body of Christ reaches maturity. During this age, we will see many amazing things happen.

After the Lord Jesus Christ became human and was raised to be a High Priest, He joined the order of Melchizedek. However, for him to join our order, Jesus had to take on both our nature and our blood. He could not do this as God. Jesus Christ had to be initiated, and we had to perform the initiation rites. This is why Jesus had to die at our hands-on Calvary before He could become part of our order. That also means that your sacrifice can never be in vain. The real question is whether you use your sacrifice correctly. Do you unintentionally make sacrifices for the purpose of your ego, like so many other things we do? Do you realize that every time you make a sacrifice, even simple ones for the kingdom, you create a prism through which you can speak, and things can be created?

You have to understand how this works. Every believer who reads this principle, I do not care how terrible they

---

21 In mathematics, a fractal is a geometric shape containing detailed structure at arbitrarily small scales, usually having a fractal dimension strictly exceeding the topological dimension. That means that any part of a whole has the same structure as the whole. (Source Wikipedia)

think they are, has made sacrifices that they have never utilized. This is because they do not understand the meaning and power of their sacrifices. In all the things they have been doing, have they purposefully looked at them as a way of speaking their intentions? Allow your mind and your words to pass through the fractalizing amplification of your sacrifices to create what is needed. The sacrifice is what will tailor your words according to the level of the need. One of our failures as pastors is that we do not teach our people. We tell them a lot about giving and it shall be given to you, but that is not what sacrifices are really for. Sacrifices create a prism, a filter, a fractalization through which your words can pass. You can say, "I want this," and the sacrifice will tailor whatever it is to the pattern it is supposed to manifest.

Look at Genesis 1. God never said, "I want an elephant." He never said, "Let there be a cow." He did not say, "Let it be an oink, oink." He never said that. God just said, "Let the earth bring forth," and that one spoken word is why you have all these species. The sacrifice allows the word to fractalize it, thereby manifesting whatever needs to be manifested from the top to the bottom. God did not have to come back to check on the word because the sacrifice will do its work.

It is important for us to remember that oftentimes, believers suffer because they do not make use of their sacrifices. It is not because they do not make sacrifices. Believers do make sacrifices. But understanding how the Melchizedek Principle works is key to understanding how God created the world and how He saved us. The same word that hung on the cross saved us and every time someone else walks through it, it saves them, too. Our salvation and experiences may be different, but it comes from that one word on the cross. And while we may call the guys who killed Jesus at Calvary evil, it was us, not the Jews or the Romans.

May the Lord bless you! You are the foundation of the world. You may quote the Bible and say that Jesus Christ is the only foundation that can be laid, but that is about the Gospel, not creation. He is the Lamb who was slain before the foundation of the world, but Jesus is not the foundation of creation. He is the Lamb.

The Lord Jesus Christ serves as the ground, while *you* are the foundation. You are planted in Jesus as the ground. You are the righteous, the foundation of worlds. Worlds, and worlds, and worlds will come out of you, not just one world. Remember, the word *"olam"* can mean "worlds." It is amazing what God has planned, but it is all because you are planted in the pre-foundation fabric of Jesus Christ. Thanks be to God who gives us the victory through Jesus Christ our Lord!

Chapter 2

THE FREQUENCY
OF SONSHIP

We are talking about how we can use Melchizedek frequencies to attain the mind of Christ in this realm. I know you may be thinking that the mind of Christ means ensuring that people do not engage in immoral acts such as fornication, theft, and lying. Good! But that is not where the mind of God and the mind of Christ start. The true mind of God and the mind of Christ are found in our perception of nature.

All of creation stems from the mind of God. For example, consider a tree and its ability to purify water. The tree is a water purification system, one containing vast amounts of water within it. Cutting down a tree means losing a lot of water. Unfortunately, modern society often ignores this fact. We need to learn about the function of trees and apply this knowledge in technology; it will lead to great wealth.

We should also study the environment and the water that is present in space, literally everywhere. Water is abundant and can be extracted from the atmosphere. Where are the Christians who are using technology to extract water from the atmosphere? Thank God for the advancements in computer science, but we need more individuals who bring spirituality into the field of science. That is the true definition of spirituality. And who should be doing that? We should be doing that. God has no issue with it.

You think you have no idea, but you do. Most believers do not understand the significance of what they carry. That is our issue. We think that what we carry is mainly for heaven. For example, when I went to Nigeria, all I heard from the churches was, "I want to make it to heaven, I want to make it to heaven!" But I say, "You have not made it in heaven yet, and that is a problem."

If you have not made it in heaven and do not have access to it, I do not know where you will go when you die. That means you have not met God. If you are just waiting to die to go to heaven, then you have not met God. To meet God, you must have access to heaven. If you do not, then wherever you are going is not heaven. At the very least, you should be aware of the presence of heaven around you, even if you cannot see it. The experience should be real to you.

What is being revealed in relation to Melchizedek has to do with the fundamental frequency of sonship as a creative technological process. We have already covered the Melchizedek Principle and its first frequency—the frequency of sacrifice. Now we move to the second frequency of the Melchizedek Principle—the frequency of sonship.

A frequency of sonship shares the fundamental nature of the first cause, which is the one who starts everything. This means you cannot be a son unless you share the intrinsic and interior nature of Divinity. You are a son because you share in the being of the one who begot you. The Melchizedek Principle carries with it the frequency of sonship. Jesus could not be a priest after the order of Melchizedek unless he was a son, but even then, Jesus could not do it if He was just the son of God. Jesus had to be the son of man. So it is a Principle of Sonship in divinity as well as in creation.

Sonship is sacrosanct, intrinsic, and fundamental in both divinity and humanity. In other words, the Melchizedek Principle has to do with the Principle of Sonship. But before we get into that, let us finish what we started in the first chapter. Melchizedek is you and me, our body. The body of Melchizedek *is* the Melchizedek body that Jesus Christ took to heaven. The Melchizedek body becomes our body because it is our robe of priesthood. Otherwise, how was Melchizedek able to give bread and wine? To do that, he had to have access to the body and blood. So where did he acquire it? Melchizedek could not have gotten the elements from himself, because he was not Jesus. Melchizedek was able to acquire the elements from the original sacrifice because the shedding of the blood and the body of the Lord Jesus Christ was not just on Calvary. Remember, there is a Lamb at the foundation, and there is blood at the foundation. It is just not the same blood as yours.

Your blood has congealed due to sin; it went from light to congelation. It is still light. However, it is thicker and has become the carrier of life,[22] but the light is still there. What is the blood that was shed before the foundation of the world? It is the very life of God, which is the light, because God is light. And by the way, that is how you are saved.

What Melchizedek gave to Abram was bread and wine. When Jesus talked about it as a physical being, He said, "This is my body, and this is my blood." Melchizedek could have it only because he had already participated in the sacrifice that leads to life, or rather, the life that leads to life. It is the sacrifice before the foundation of the world. Melchizedek had something from the fabric upon which the foundations are laid.

When you take communion, Jesus says, "Remember me." It is a reconstitution of His being as the fabric of pre-creation, the pre-foundation of the universe. That means you are reconstituting the original principle of divinity and fundamentally changing creation by taking communion.

The book of Hebrews begins by comparing Jesus to angels and repeatedly uses the word *sons*. It ends in chapter eight with Melchizedek, which indicates a fundamental principle. You cannot be a High Priest in the order of Melchizedek nor have the Melchizedek Principle without participating in sonship. Jesus could not be a priest after the order of Melchizedek until he participated in the sonship of humanity. In becoming a son of man, Jesus is becoming you. To do so, Jesus must bring His divinity into who He is, or else Jesus becoming you will not change you. When Jesus brings His

22 *See* Leviticus 17:11 For the life of the flesh is in the blood...

divinity into you at the moment He becomes you, it creates a complementarity where Jesus becomes you, and you become Jesus. It is a dual sonship with Jesus being both a Son of God and a Son of man. By joining himself to Melchizedek, Melchizedek is brought back to humanity, making humanity no longer just a creature. This decision by God determines that a human being can move from being a creature to being uncreated.

Do you remember John chapter three? It is a very simple passage that states you must be born from above. That which is born of God *is* God, and what is born of the flesh *is* flesh. What is born of the Spirit *is* spirit. In other words, if you are born of God, you immediately cease being a creature. If you are born of Adam, you are a creature.

I want to mess with some of your theology. Your children did not come from heaven. This is a Western theology, but it is not true. Your children's DNA comes from Adam. In fact, even their soul comes from Adam. They must be born from above before they can come from heaven. Only a believer in Jesus Christ comes from heaven. Children are innocent and thus have no activated sin in their being. That does not mean they come from heaven. The Spirit of the Lord may rest upon them, but they are not from heaven. They are from Earth, because every human being is of earth and is earthly.[23] Again, your children did not come from heaven; they are part of Adam's children. I know that some people may have a problem with this, as they believe that a child's innocence means they must come from heaven. But, innocence actually means inactivated sin. This is why I am a theologian; I do not rely on sentimentality.

Notice that I did not say that your children are going to hell. I said that their sin is not activated, which is exactly

23 John 3:31

why there is a place in heaven for children who die before their sins are activated. They are taught until they make a decision. This is the problem with Universalism. Every human being must make a decision, even those who never heard the Gospel in this world. When they meet Jesus and the cloud of witnesses who testify to them, they must make a choice and say yes or no. Some people will look Jesus in the face and say no. The notion that everyone will automatically believe when they see Jesus is a lie straight from hell. The satan and his system saw the glory of God in heaven, not on earth, and they cried, "Holy, Holy, Holy." They were cherubs overlooking the mystery of divinity and saw the depths of God. But, they still turned against Him.

When somebody tells you that everyone is going to be saved, it is because they do not understand the sovereignty of man and the foundational principle of what it means to be human. The essence of being human is having a free will that is able to say no to God. God does not have a problem with human free will, and He does not have a problem with your free will. That is because God does not want to relate to slaves—He wants kings. A king without free will is not a king. You can listen to all that nonsense, but in theology, we call it Universalism. If somebody tells you it is not Universalism, they are lying and do not know theology. You cannot find any passages in Scripture that talk about the restoration of all men. Let me point something out to you. The Bible talks about the restoration of all things,[24] not all people. You are *not* a thing.

I am writing about sonship now, and that is why I am addressing this issue. You need to understand who you are. You need to remove some of this nonsense so you can be clear about your own identity and sovereignty. When you realize

---

24 Matthew 17:11; Mark 9:12; Acts 3:21; Ephesians 4:10

that God gave you this sovereign will, He said to you, "You make the decision; I submit to your will."

How exactly did you become a believer? You believe with your heart and confess with your mouth that Jesus Christ is Lord.[25] God subjected Himself to what was going on in your heart and what you said with your mouth. The same method gets your prayers answered. You ask, and God responds.

Why do people always try to defend God and fix His character? They say, "God is so loving He will not let anyone go to hell." But love allows people to be who they want to be. If you say that you love people, you will always be with them and support them, even though they disagree with you. You will even let them do what they want to do, even though it causes you pain. But you say, "No, God cannot do that." Why not? When you say that, it means your nature is different from God's.

This is a real problem. The Bible says that all creation is subjected, right? It was not creation that subjected itself, but God who subjected creation to futility.[26] God did not subject *man* to futility. Once you get this theology wrong, you start talking nonsense. You are not just creation; you are one who is created in the image and likeness of God. When man fell, God brought all of creation into a lower state. You have never seen a cricket in its real nature. You have never seen an elephant, tiger, lion, or antelope in their true nature. You have never seen a tree in its actual nature either. You only see creation in the way God made it so you could handle it. What you have seen is a diminished being. God did that, so you could handle them in your fallen state. You have never even seen a river in its full force. There is nothing currently in creation that you have ever seen in its true nature. The sun

25 Romans 10:9
26 Romans 8:20

is not even shining in His full power, and neither is the moon. The stars are so far removed that you cannot reach most of them because of your fall. The one time God allowed the ocean and waters to react in accordance with their nature, the whole earth was inundated. Why does the Bible call the locust an army of God?[27] You have never seen the locust in its real nature.

Think about this. The Bible says that on that day, the sun will be seven times brighter,[28] and the moon will be as bright as the sun.[29] Which day is Scripture talking about? It is telling us about the day the restoration of creation happens. However, the restoration of creation will not happen unless we reach our true level of sonship.

I have heard it said that Scripture now teaches that man was subjected to futility. That is *not* true. Man fell by free will. That is exactly why he needs repentance. On the other hand, animals are more righteous and holy than man since they have never committed sin or disobeyed God. This is why animals can be used for sacrifice, but man cannot.

To atone for man's sin, God needed a person without sin in their blood system. Many people blindly accept this idea without fully thinking it through. They may be sentimental about salvation because a relative died without accepting Jesus, but salvation does not mean everyone must be saved. Some people even believe that they can go into hell to save their relatives, but this actually makes them unrighteous. Jesus did not die to save only His relatives. Therefore, if someone saves only their relatives, it means they are unrighteous.

Do you see why transformation is so important? Even when we start to act in a spiritual manner, we still act based

27 Joel 2:1-11, 25
28 Isaiah 30-26
29 Song of Songs 6:10

on selfishness and emotions. People want to bring their grandpa out of hell without considering others. You get all the power you say you have, but you only use it to save your grandpa and leave everyone else's relatives behind. This is not a biblical or theological movement—it is a sentimental one. People are claiming to take Christians to spaceships. Is this really what Christianity is about? Or is it just another New Age idea? God Almighty, Jesus, help us!

Why is creation so important that God had to subject it? If God had not subjected creation, it would rule over you. It has never been God's intention for anything to rule over you, and that includes the angels. Angels cannot rule over you; they are not allowed to do so. You were created by original divine intent to be a son. Otherwise, Jesus would not call himself Son of man and Son of God." The whole purpose of creating man was for sonship.

In the original sacrifice of the Lamb, Melchizedek affirmed His sonship, thereby making it possible for God to be involved as a human being whenever He chooses. Romans 8:19 says that all creation is groaning and mourning for the manifestation of the sons of God. That means they are waiting for you; they cannot be restored unless sons are manifested.

It is funny how some people reject Scripture, only picking the parts they like. They ignore the verses they do not like and move on to the next one. But you have to look at the whole of Scripture together. You must have both a Scripture and a canon. I, as an Ethiopian Christian, have 88 books in my Bible.

If you have a biblical canon, we judge you by it. People are rejecting the idea of a biblical canon, and they are talking about it as if it does not exist. But there is a canon, and if you tell me you are a Protestant Christian, I will judge your ideas based on the 66 books of your canon.[30]

I need a ground for conversation, and that is what the biblical canon provides. Just like in the USA, we always refer back to the Constitution. If you want to argue about your freedom, you must have a common reference point. If you tell me I am not an American, I will refer back to the Constitution and tell you I am just as American as you are, regardless of how I got here.

The same principle applies to our beliefs. We need an objective text to see where we stand. It is foolish to argue without a common reference point. If it is just your experience, I can never really engage in a meaningful conversation with you. If you come to me and say God spoke to you, I do not have anything to say because you are not allowing me to analyze your experience. How would I stand up to you if God says something? Then you are putting me in trouble with God. My wife always says that when someone comes and says, "God said," she steps back. I am okay with God. I do not want to get into trouble with Him. This is what Christians use as an excuse not to be critiqued. Then you are better than God, because even He says, "Come let us reason together."[31] This is my Jewish side. We debate. We even put God in a chair and ask Him questions.

"Okay, God, why did you say that?" He may never give us an answer, but we do it anyway. I do not have a problem asking God questions. I do not have a problem fighting with God. I love Him dearly; He is my life, my everything. But sometimes there are things He says to me that lead me to

---

30 A biblical canon is a set of texts (also called «books») which a particular Jewish or Christian religious community regards as part of the Bible. The English word canon comes from the Greek κανών kanōn, meaning «rule» or «measuring stick» (Source Wikipedia).

31 Isaiah 1:18

argue with Him. Come on! I am a Jew! We have to have a conversation about this. He wins all the time, but that is not the point.

You are coming into sonship and it is important. Sonship is in the nature of the Godhead and it is eternal. That is why a man can be nothing other than the Son of God. That is why Luke 3 ends with "and Adam was a Son of God." It is about sonship.

This brings me to my next point—the Melchizedek Principle is not about being the wife of God. You are not a bride; you are a son. There is a bride, but it is not you. You have a problem because homosexuality is spreading, and you are responsible. You may call it a metaphor, but that is the root of your problem. Churches are now arguing that they are the real bride of Christ, but they do not understand what it means to be married. I said this 20 years ago, but no one listened. I told you to change the bridal paradigm because it is not scriptural. You do not have to read any more of my books, but I am still going to tell you the truth. I dare you to find a Scripture that says you are the wife of Christ. I dare you to find one verse that does not use a conditional adjective or adverb. Where in the Bible does it say you are the bride of Christ?

In Ephesians 5, Paul says that you should love your wife as Christ loved the church and gave Himself up, but he does not say that Christ is married to the church. You are the one who drew that conclusion. It is not in the text. Jews who went to Europe and learned the European pagan ways brought this idea back to Israel and told us that God has a wife. But African Jews and Jews in India do not say that. It is a European problem.

The Western Church, which has the greatest problem with homosexuality, is the one that argues that the church is the

bride of Christ. They have sissy men who dance like women in the church and say, "I am the bride of Christ." Really? Why does he say that? The Melchizedek Principle is about sonship, not about being a wife.

You have already corrupted Scripture because Jesus said that people will neither marry nor be given in marriage at the resurrection.[32] You have taken the concept of marriage from earth and imposed it onto heaven, but Jesus specifically said that this does not happen. I can show you the text that says you are a son, but can you show me a text that says you are a wife? I understand that some of you may be getting offended, but that is not my intention. The point I am making is that the Melchizedek Principle is all about sonship. If you make yourself a wife, then you are always subservient and can never be like God. Why? Because a wife does not share the same DNA as her husband, except for the first woman who was created. You cannot use that metaphor to describe yourself. If you do, you will not inherit anything and can be divorced.

Allow me to push the metaphor further. The Principle of Sonship is an eternal principle. That means that all are called sons of God in heaven. When women are saying that they have the same issue with being a son, remember that Adam was created first. God created man first and then brought the woman into existence because it is easier for you to return to the wholeness that you were in the beginning than to believe in this separation.

The biblical teachings are clear. I understand it can be difficult, but if the Bible said I was a bride, I would have to reconsider my beliefs as a Christian. I came to this realization because I was arguing with homosexuals who claimed they understood the concept better than I did. They were quoting

32 Matthew 22:30

passages that said men were the bride of Christ, and I was saying that the Bible does not actually say that. It is hard to argue with them when that is what the church has been teaching for so long.

However, it is not just homosexuality being affected by this misinterpretation. It also explains why some of our daughters are not getting married. When a woman believes she is already married, men do not see her as a single woman. It is a spiritual thing; their soul perceives her as already being married. Look at the number of young women in the church who are not married yet consider themselves married to Jesus. Who would want to compete with Jesus for a wife? This notion causes men to shy away. I see this all over the world: young women saying, "Why cannot they see me?" They cannot because you are already married.

Unfortunately, many of the young women who consider themselves married to Jesus also become arrogant when it comes to dealing with men. Most men will agree here. This is how men walk, with their eyes. They know a woman who is available just by looking. You think being married to Christ does not cover you, but it does. You are a married woman, and your whole mentality is that of a woman who is married. Think about it. Check your life and see.

Once I started removing that from the women in my church, I started seeing more people get married. Men look at women and see them as available. I like it. Sisters, if you make the man not want to look at the woman, how are you going to get married?

Here is another thing. The majority of abortions are committed by people who go to church. Most people do not know that, but it is a big part of why the Christian population is dwindling. these so-called Christian women who go to church who are having abortions. Muslim women do not do it. It is a deep spiritual thing. You are not a wife; you are a son. Let me help you with this. We all accept that Adam was the Son of God, right? And Exodus 24 says, "Israel is my firstborn Son." You see the reference over and over again—sons of Israel, sons of Israel, sons of Israel, sons of Israel, sons of Israel. You can say it is a patriarchal society, but I beg to differ. There is a reason for the statement: "You are my Son; today I have begotten you." It means, "You share in my inheritance. You will never be removed, divorced, or kicked out. You will always be with me." God gave His only Son sonship. And for those of you thinking about the 10 virgins, let me explain.

Your culture may not understand the Jewish and African cultures, but the 10 virgins are actually the friends of the bride. In African cultures, when a man marries, the wife's friends come around her to protect her. Likewise, the friends of the bridegroom come and surround the bridegroom. At midnight, they go get the bride and her friends are singing. It is a game of courtship.

The 10 virgins were supposed to be there for their friend, the bride, and convince the bridegroom to take her. They were supposed to follow the bride's heart to the bridegroom's house. The fact that they left at night means that they were not disciplined, and thus could not come back in. They were not the bride; they were just bridesmaids. Otherwise, the bridegroom would be marrying 10 women! The bridegroom takes his bride and the bridesmaids into his house. They are supposed to go with them.

I remember marriages in Nigeria. The friends went for about a week to try to get the bride to leave her father's house. The game was to get her friends to open the door for the bridegroom. The day they finally let him in, they all

danced together. All the friends joined in and they all went home to celebrate the marriage.

This is simple stuff, but you know a lot of people think African culture is demonic. They typically would not think that Africans can do that sort of thing. The truth is, Jewish culture is actually African culture. The West divided the Middle East. They created the Middle East away from Africa. The Middle East is a creation of the West. Originally, it did not exist as its own region. It was northeast Africa until it was re-zoned by the West and called the Middle East. I only mention this so that you have the context.

Returning to the bridegroom story, it is not about the 10 virgins and it is certainly not about the bridegroom marrying those girls. It is about them being the friends of the bride. Are you the brother or sister of the bridegroom, or are you the wife of the bridegroom? What does Jesus call you? He calls you, "My relative." Jesus said,

"‹...I am ascending to my Father and your Father, to my God and your God.'"[33]

By being born from above, you now share the same blood with the Lord Jesus Christ. You are still thinking, "But what about all those passages in the book of Revelation?" The final passage says,

"Come, I will show you the Bride, the wife of the Lamb."[34]

33 John 20:17b
34 Revelation 21:9

Do not ignore what the next verse says.

"And he carried me away in the Spirit to a great, high mountain, and showed me the holy city Jerusalem coming down out of heaven from God,"[35]

So, who exactly is the wife of Jesus? Not you. If you were born from above, then there must be a womb from where you came, correct? It is in the Bible, by the way. Galatians 4 says there are two women—one above and one below. One is a slave and the other is free. The final verse of that passage says,

"But the Jerusalem above is free, and she is our mother." [36]

You have a mother and no, you cannot be your own mother. Your mother is above, and she is a city. It is in your Bible.

Whether or not you like the pagan language, the earth is the mother principle. Sonship works like this: you share the same image and the same rulership. God could have made it a daughter, but He did not. God said it was a son, although it is not about gender really. It is about inheritance. I am not saying women are less. This is simply the way God set up the process.

The problem is that we are not reading Scripture correctly. There comes a time when our gender, not gender confusion, will disappear. Scripture tells us there will be neither male nor female. We are making gender the thing that will determine how we are in heaven, and it is just not so. We even want to create female angels when there is neither male nor female in

---

35 Revelation 21:10
36 Galatians 4:21-31

heaven. We do this because we think this earthbound state is how it will be forever. No!

Have you seen yourself in the spirit? Have you ever left your body? Have you noticed how some of the most important parts of your body that differentiate gender are not there? It is amazing how, when your body becomes a light body, everything that you thought was important disappears. That is how I know when people have never really seen themselves in the spirit.

The pattern of earth was set for the increase of humanity so that potential gods could be born into creation. This means that when you have a child, you have just given birth to a potential god. The thing you carry is a god in potential. Your baby was a god in seed form. It is such a powerful thing, but it is in the Bible.

I said, "You are gods, sons of the Most High, all of you."[37]

Let us come back to the topic of sonship. To understand this concept, we must learn through Jesus Christ. Let us look at who Jesus Christ is, because by understanding His identity as a Son, we will begin to see ourselves in a different light. We are not different sons. When people say that we are adopted sons, they need to read the passage again. The passage actually refers to the adoption of our bodies.[38] Our bodies are redeemed and adopted into the Godhead, and this is what we are waiting for. We are waiting for our bodies to be adopted into divinity because we are already sons. We are

37 Psalms 82:6
38 Romans 8:23

born sons from above. God does not have a body, so He must adopt our body into His divinity.

This is what the Scripture actually says. We groan, waiting for the adoption of our bodies. Whether this occurs now, through immediate transportation, or even when we die and are resurrected, God adopts the human body into the Godhead. It is clearly stated in Scripture.

You are a son, which means you are birthed by God. You are cut from the very pillar of God's being. God released you from Himself. There is no distinction between you and Him. But this did not happen just because you are a human being. It happened because you said "Yes."

By your voice, you activated your own birth from the depths of the being of God. You activated your birth by faith and by voice, by heart and by voice. The real voice that transmutes you is yours. How long did it take you to get saved? Can you show me? It may have taken you a while to fully grasp the reality of it, but your salvation did not happen over five years. If it did, we need to re-evaluate your understanding. When you said yes to the Father, the Father did not wait until the next day. What did He do? Father God saved you instantly. Furthermore, He did it through your voice! Your existence was immediately transmuted from a human being into a god.

God is waiting for your voice. Specifically, He is waiting for your voice to align with your heart. Then, in the twinkling of an eye, He transmutes you. The word in 1 Thessalonians 4:17 for "in the air" is the same as the word "Spirit."[39] God is waiting to hear a certain frequency come out of your voice. This frequency transmutes and changes you. If we, as God's children, can reach that frequency, our bodies can

39 1 Thessalonians 4:17

be immediately transmuted. Scientists are discovering that everything is a frequency. If we can find the resonance and frequency of something, we can either enhance it or destroy it.

Scientists do not yet understand why we grow old (called senescence) nor why a cell simply shuts down and its voice disappears.[40] They do not know why we die. But when the frequency disappears, the cell does not move anymore; it just stops. Scientists are trying to figure out a way to reactivate the cell when it stops.

I think it is in the sound because that is what the Bible says in 1 Thessalonians:

For the Lord himself will descend from heaven with a cry of command, with the voice of an archangel, and with the sound of the trumpet of God.

Not all of us will die, but we shall all be changed. However, was it the voice of an angel that got you saved? No. It was your voice. When the voice of the body of Christ is united, and we become one voice, something will happen to our bodies. I do not know what the sound is, but I know it resides somewhere. The universe was created by word, by sound. Light is sound. Life is sound. Love is sound. As sons, the voice of God has now been embedded in us.

Sonship is eternal in nature because it is a part of the Godhead. It is not something that occurred in the linear confines of time. In other words, when God was God, and when God became God, at the moment that God began being God—which is forever and eternally—that is when sonship immediately emerged. It did not emerge after God became God. Sonship emerged at the immediate and eternal moment of the inception of Divinity. Sonship is intrinsic to

40   https://en.wikipedia.org/wiki/Senescence

the very nature of God. So then sonship is a reflection of God's openness to everything that comes along. God has this nature.

The spirit is also a possibility, and God is spirit. What is spirit? Spirit is something that cannot be contained in a particular form or structure. Spirit is something that can enter any system and become what it touches, transmuting it. In other words, God is an open system. I am not talking only about God's character, but also about how He relates to the universe. God loves you so much that He meets you where you are and becomes what you need. For example, when you eat every day, you may think you are just eating food. In reality, God becomes the food that you eat.

Ultimately, this means that you live in a sacramental universe, one where God provides for you and becomes your sustenance. He adjusts according to your needs. Your preacher has already told you that God will meet you at the point of your need and become the solution to your need. His essence becomes what you need because God loves you that much. God does not have a problem with you consuming Him because it does not cause Him to diminish. In fact, your consumption of His being actually draws you back into God. He is willing to give Himself to you.

Sonship is a Biblical principle. When the early church first began to describe who Jesus is, they struggled to find the right words. Do you know what they did? They repeated certain phrases repeatedly, such as, "He is a Son begotten, not created (or made)." Adam, on the other hand, was formed. He is referred to as a son, but he was formed. However, Christ is begotten; He was not formed nor made. The early church used phrases such as, "Very God of very God, very life of very life, light from light, glory from glory"[41] to describe the

---

41   The Nicene Creed: https://rts.edu/historical-creeds-of-faith/the-nicene-creed/

Lord Jesus Christ. So then everything that God is, the Son is. When Jesus was in the Godhead, He was simply God. We call him Jesus from our perspective, but in the Godhead, He was just God.

Sonship was God's original intention. The second person of the Trinity took on this role because a Son must share the nature of the one who begets him. Sonship is what God desires; it is the inner principle of divinity that is made manifest. This means that the being that died before the foundation of the world was both a Son and a full embodiment of the heart of Divinity. When the Son was crucified, killed, and slain as a Lamb, God was fully present in him.

So how did God become a being that is a Son? In order to create a world that God knew might rebel against Him, He had to manifest the Principle of Sonship. And for this to happen, there had to be a fundamental Principle of Love, an outpouring of compassion before anything even existed. For this to be possible, the being who was making this motion had to be complete in and of Himself. Love is not just what you give to people—it is also what you are in yourself. The foundation of the universe is light and love is a part of that foundation. So for this being to emit light, there had to be a source of that light. And that light must be the being of God. This means that light must be fully indwelling in this One so that the light, love, and life will go through the prism of His life and be manifested in everything throughout creation.

Creation is the result of the inner movement of Divinity. When love, life, and light are combined, the outcome is ecstatic joy. Creation flows out of ecstatic joy. Creation produces because it came from the depth of God when the three persons of the Godhead were in interaction with love, light, and life.

When the Lamb was laid on the altar before the foundation of the world, it was an expression of the fullness of Divinity lying in nothingness. When this happened, the Godhead spoke. Because it was a revelation and an embodiment of what was inside, They spoke forth the fullness of Divinity. This means that it is possible for creation to continue on to infinity because the foundation and pre-foundation is God himself.

What Melchizedek did was to release the nature of God into an empty space so that the world could exist.[42] This is what you and I did (as Melchizedek represents humanity), but what Father God did was release the Son, literally manifesting the Principle of Sonship into creation as the fullness of God. This was necessary because the Son, the One who carries the DNA of the fullness of the Father, also serves as the reason why the environment is protected from the inner power of the Creator. The death of the Lord Jesus Christ before the foundation of the world protects the world from being destroyed. His death protects the creation from the complete influence and relationship with God, the culmination of which would cause all creation to return to the Godhead.

If we related to God the way God is without the Son serving as the boundary of creation, all of us would cease to exist and enter into a divine state of being, returning to our original position in the Godhead.[43] There would be no relationship. The Son, the Lord Jesus Christ, who serves as the pre-foundation substrate, also serves as the protective

---

42 This is described as the principle of Tzimtzum
   https://www.chabad.org/library/article_cdo/aid/361884/jewish/Tzimtzum.htm
43 1 Corinthians 15:28

principle, the corona of creation that keeps it from running back into Divinity. The sacrifice of the Son is what allows us to experience God in a way that we can handle, and with love.

When we talk about wanting to see God, to experience all of Him, we do not actually know what we are asking. Do not get me wrong, "Open the Eyes of My Heart" is a great song with awesome lyrics,[44] but we really have no clue what we are asking. If the Principle of Sonship did not surround creation, we would literally disappear completely into God and lose our unique identity. We would quite literally disappear and cease to live.

God allows us to have a reflexive relationship with Him. Sonship is the foundation of this relationship, creating an interrelation where God looks at us, and we look at Him. God's whole purpose is to see Himself in us. However, the reflexive relationship we experience now is not the same as it was in the pre-foundation.

When God looked into the foundation of the Son embodying Him, God saw a reflection of Himself. When God spoke to the pre-foundation, it gave God what He desired. This was because the pre-foundation reflected creation back to Him. Let us call the Son, Jesus Christ, for now. If you were there, you would not have known Him as Jesus Christ. You would have known Him simply as the Son, the God who became the pre-foundation substrate of creation. That is why when the angels sang, they did not say, "Oh thou Son of God." They said, "But thou, oh Lord."

He was a son, but they did not say, "Son." Those angels did not say, "Jesus." They said, "but thou, oh Lord." The sons of Korah spoke of this when they referenced the one who laid down his life. They said, "...your throne is forever and ever

44   https://www.azlyrics.com/lyrics/michaelwsmith/opentheeyesofmyheart.html

and ever."[45] And when God brought the first-begotten into the world, you may think that was only when the Lord Jesus Christ was born in Bethlehem, but no! When God created the world, the Bible says that the angels rejoiced. When God brought forth the Son, the first-begotten into the world, the angels rejoiced! Wisdom rejoiced! Everything rejoiced![46]

The Principle of Sonship and sharing of nature are repeated and reiterated in every creation, including the new creation. The DNA of the person we call the Son upholds every iteration of creation. Remember, everything is held up by the Lord Jesus Christ[47] who is the fullness of God, a Son. The Son, the second person of the Godhead, embodies the complete fullness of God.[48] Everything in this universe flows through Jesus Christ.

What if I told you that the events in creation were the reason Adam was created? What if the reason you were saved was so God could speak through you to create the possibility for worlds to come into existence? I tell you now, it is based on the same Principle of Sonship. Either you are a son, or you are not a son. If you are a son, then your life can be used as a fractalizing prism for God's Word to manifest levels of creation. But it is much more than just you being a son.

Do you see the Lord Jesus Christ, the Son? Both His pre-creation reality and His in-creation reality are a picture of your life. I do not want to push you too hard because I know your mind is already racing and it is possible that your cognitive system may reject some of what I am saying. So allow me to try again. You are either a son, or you are not a son. If the Son appeared in pre-creation to serve as the pre-

---

45 Psalm 45:6
46 Proverbs 8:31
47 Colossians 1:15-20
48 Colossians 2:9

foundation of the worlds that now exist, what does that say about you once you become a son in fullness?

Let me quote a simple message from Scripture: "You will rule worlds." However, if you read the New Testament from a Hebrew perspective, it would read like this: 'The righteous are the foundation of worlds,[49] not just that, you will also judge angels.'[50] You might be thinking that judging angels means that you are going to sit in the corner while all the angels come to you, and you will say, "You did not do what you were supposed to do." No. The word "judge" can also mean to rule and have dominion.

But if you are not a son, what then? We cannot continue thinking in such a limited way. Let me ask you a question. Why did God create the whole world? So far in the universe that we know right now, we have three hundred billion galaxies and countless more in the dark world have not yet been discovered. Who would do that unless they had a plan?

We often say that we are going to judge the fallen angels; the problem with that is, they have already been judged and their sentence passed. So, what is the Bible referring to here? You are going to judge the righteous, meaning you will rule and direct.

Judgment involves the capacity and willingness to put things in order. Judgment is about putting things in the right place. If you take the root word "mishpat"[51] and consider the root word for family, "mishap," it refers to the structuring of a household. This means that if you are a son, you will have a house to rule.

Jesus hinted at this when He talked about the parable of talents. You will rule over ten cities, or five, but we tend to

49 Proverbs 10:25
50 1 Corinthians 6:3 https://Biblehub.com/greek/2919.htm
51 https://tinyurl.com/35ydawks

think that this means we will have control over New York or New Delhi. No. The Lord Jesus Christ was talking about worlds.[52]

The truth is, you cannot really handle thinking about what God has in mind for you. If we are talking about being a son, we need to start thinking in a new way. Remember, all of creation is waiting for your manifestation.[53]

That means Jupiter will not be what it is supposed to be until you show up. All the galaxies, such as the one drawing our galaxy into itself, will be doing what they are doing until you and I arrive. As sons, we need to start thinking more broadly than just telling the devil to sit down and expecting him to do so. In actuality, we will organize angels according to their patterns in the world that you rule.

Let me start by addressing a commonly held fallacy. The world is *not* shrinking; it is expanding! In other words, the universe is creating evermore space for an ever-increasing number of manifestations of worlds. The question is, to whom do these worlds belong? Angels will not rule them because God never intended for angels to rule them. Father God intended for human beings to rule them. The Bible states that God did not subject the world to come to angels,[54] but to us. This makes me laugh at those who tell me that they want to preach to angels. It has nothing to do with angels! God's intention is for flesh and blood to rule, but not just any flesh and blood. God's divine intent is toward flesh and blood that has become transformed, where the body has become translucent and the blood has become pure light once again. When a human being has taken on the light body and has become a reflection of Divinity, they become the

---

52 other cities too will be mothers of new worlds.

53 Romans 8:19

54 Hebrews 2:5

fullness of light; this allows them to rule and enables them to become the light of the world.

We are the light of the world! So, when you start singing, "This Little Light of Mine," remember that is not what the Bible tells you. You are truly the light of the world. Furthermore, you will be the light of a greater world, because that is what the Father wants. Just think of how great God is!

God says you will be a ruler. If you are thinking, "Yeah, I'm going to rule," do not just focus on ruling a small village on the side of the bush. Think bigger. That small settlement is not what God is talking about. God does not really talk that way. If He talks small, it is because there is something big. If God says to you, "I want you to do this small thing," do not ever think that God is just interested in a small thing. That is because there is always something bigger. This is what most Christians forget. God did not create you to sit in the corner and take part in a small thing. Father God created entire galaxies with you in mind when He made you a son.

How else is God supposed to show you what you are going to look like, except by sending the Son from within the Godhead and using Jesus as a pattern and paradigm? Do not get me wrong, I love that Christian way of speaking. But, I think that sometimes we do not fully grasp it. Why do you say, "I want to be like Christ; I want to be like my big brother?" Do you really think that being everything the Lord Jesus Christ is means that you will not steal a cookie from the store? Not stealing a cookie from the store is bigger than the cookie itself. But that single act of self-restraint does not make you like Jesus. What makes you like Jesus is the fact that you do not steal the cookie because you have the power to create millions of cookies. That is just a metaphor for those who like cookies. But for me, being a son means that I always go back to the Lord Jesus Christ.

Let us examine Jesus' pre-existence, His pre-incarnate life, what the Scriptures say about Jesus, and then let us look at His life on earth. Did you know that the Bible actually says that a time will come when Jesus will give up everything?[55] This means that the sacrifice that the Lord Jesus Christ made as a Son makes it possible for you to also become a son. It is not just what He did but also *why* the Lord Jesus Christ did it that is so important. When you come into your sonship, Jesus will return to the Father and say, "I am coming back. Let them do what it is you want them to do." This passage always discomforts Christians, as it says that Jesus will return to God and God will be "all in all."[56] But why would Jesus return to God and give up everything? Who is the messiah giving it up for?

The Bible begins by calling you a son.[57] The second person of the Trinity has left His name in creation through everything He has done. By calling upon His name, the name of the Lord Jesus Christ, you can reconstitute Jesus in creation and perform an anamnesis.[58] Jesus can manifest in creation, but His ultimate goal is to return to the Godhead so that the Godhead remains intact with humanity serving as the fourth dimension of Divinity.

Jesus took a body into heaven with Him. Whose body is it? It is yours! Remember, you are called the body of Christ.[59] The body sitting there is actually a Melchizedek body because it was made for Jesus. And guess what? It was

---

55 1 Corinthians 15:24
56 1 Corinthians 15:28
57 The first word of the Bible begins with a Beth, which is an image of sonship
58 Anamnesis: A recalling to memory by the mind
59 1 Corinthians 15:28

made for *all* the sons. This body of Melchizedek is the body of light, translucent, able to move through anything, capable of infinitely multiplying itself, and enabling omnipresent manifestations. You are seated in heavenly places.[60] That is a plural statement—you are not in just one place. Wherever Jesus is, you are.

The issue is not that you are not there but rather, your consciousness has not been raised to the point where you have become aware enough. Being a son means following the pattern laid out by the second person of the Godhead, the Lord Jesus Christ, on earth. The things that Jesus did on earth served as a pointer to who God is and who we are in God. It might surprise you to know that healing was not just about healing the body. In truth, the reason for healing the body was that the body is the cosmic chamber of Divinity.

Have you ever asked yourself, "Why does God care about my body?" God cares about your body because He made it for Himself. It is the only thing in creation with His fingerprints. The body is the only thing God made with His own hands. Everything else, Father God spoke into existence with His Word.

Father God made your body with His hands to make it expansive enough to contain Himself. Do you realize that not even the universe or the worlds of the worlds can contain God? Yet God made your little body with such care and attention to detail to enable it to contain Him. The fullness of God can live in you. The whole issue of this Sonship is much more powerful than we have yet to understand. You and I are sons in ways that we are still trying to grasp. The Bible says, "In Jesus Christ, the fullness of the Godhead dwelt bodily."[61] So if my body is the temple of the Holy Spirit, it

60 Ephesians 2:6
61 Colossians 2:9

means that God is trying to make my body able to handle the fullness of God.

Father God did not just send Jesus into the world to save me from sin, although that is a foundational aspect. Father sent Jesus to teach me who I am and what I can be. When I look at the Lord Jesus Christ, I see what I am supposed to be like. Sonship is the foundation of this, not "wife-ship." Do not misunderstand me here. Marriage is amazing but only once you understand the principle of being a son of God. Only then will you understand the importance of your marriage.

You are giving God bodies[62] that will ultimately become light bodies where God will dwell. Mankind has such a significant role to play. When people tell me they do not want to have children, I cringe. Let me put it this way, if I knew what I know now, I would have had 10 children, because every human being that is born is a harbinger of worlds. I say that it is wrong to stop having children because now I truly understand what children are. Western education made me believe that children are just a cost, but now I understand these little creatures will become gods one day. They will become sons, true manifestations of Divinity. I am raising my grandchildren as if they will become another god, potential gods. I hope you understand that it is we who dislike the body—not God. We know we fail, but God has always focused on making our body immortal in order to enable it to become a light bearer because our body is His very own house. That is what we find with the begotten Son, the first Son, our older brother, our Lord, and our Master. The Lord Jesus Christ is our God, but Jesus chose to be made

---

62 Romans 12:1-3

flesh and blood because He wants us to be partakers so that we can become unmitigated partakers of Divinity like Him.

The frequency of Sonship is what comes up when you think of Melchizedek. You begin to think of what it means to be a son. That is because the first interaction that Melchizedek has is with Sonship. Melchizedek is a body that was made for us, one that we lost when Adam fell. The capacity to transmute that body into the Melchizedek Principle was lost. The Lord Jesus Christ came to restore that access. Therefore, part of the reason Jesus is a High Priest after the order of Melchizedek is to keep that body intact forever. However, you cannot forget the verse that says,

When all things are subjected to him, then the Son himself will also be subjected to him who put all things in subjection under him, that God may be all in all.

[63]Paul then proceeds to talk about our own resurrection. God does all these things to enable the full manifestation of our Sonship. We do not know all the mysteries, but ultimately, you and I are supposed to become a full embodiment of Divinity. God is supposed to look at us and see not just our potential to look like Him, but to actually see us as Himself!

The Frequency of Sonship derives from the very sound of the being of God. This is the reason Melchizedek is a higher priest than Aaron was. The Melchizedek Priesthood is greater than the Aaronic Priesthood specifically because it is a priesthood connected to Sonship. The Melchizedek Priesthood is original in the sense that it comes directly from God. Jesus did not just become a Son within the Godhead; God created a being that became the Son in creation. Nonetheless, before that being could be manifested in creation, that Son, the Lord Jesus Christ, had to give His life.

63 1 Corinthians 15:28, 42-57

Adam is the result of the Son of God, who died before the foundation of the world. Even His creation could not happen without the Lamb having been slain before the foundation of the world.

> **And because you are sons, God has sent the Spirit of his Son into our hearts, crying, "Abba! Father!" So you are no longer a slave, but a son, and if a son, then an heir through God.**[64]

Everything the Lord Jesus Christ inherits, we also inherit. Yet, as we keep passing on, we forget the Principle of Sacrifice.

---

64   Galatians 4:6-7

Chapter 3

THE FREQUENCY
OF FREE WILL

I know that this topic might cause some people to get offended. If you are one of them, just ignore it and glean from my words what will benefit you. If that is the only skill you learn, I promise that it will help benefit you in many aspects of your life. That said, I will still challenge you on what I believe are some terrible and wrong doctrines. I am going to begin by diving deeper into Universalism. If Universalism is true, then God will have to apologize to Adam and Eve and to Israel for punishing them both for being disobedient. And then, all of the Israelites who are scattered throughout the world, especially those whom God said shall be cut off from Israel and shall never return, must receive apologies. If there is no freedom of choice, then God is a liar and must even apologize to humanity for giving us a false choice.

If you want to believe in this Universalism nonsense, you can keep doing so, but you need to understand exactly what you are saying. When you speak about Universalism, you are talking about taking away God's gift of freedom to man. The devil is the only one who can tell you that you have a choice when you do not. If God told us we had a choice when we did not, then God is a liar. I desperately want to address this issue, because it is a doctrine from the pit of hell and it is certainly not a Christian doctrine.

If you choose to follow this type of doctrine, then do not call yourself a Christian. If you follow Universalism, you also have to remove the sacred perspective of Scripture.

For God so loved the world that he gave his only Son, that whoever believes in him should not perish but have eternal life.[65]

The fact is that not everyone believes. As Paul says, some people do not have faith.[66]

The fundamental issue is that human beings have a responsibility. Otherwise, how could we be divine if God has never given us a choice? How else can we make any decision that is truly our own if He wants to make us gods? The Scriptures are clear on this point. Two tribes of Israel were completely lost because God cut them off from Israel. Then the Gentiles came in and thought that God would not do the same to them. Does God change? The only change here is that God gave Gentiles an opportunity to believe.

The grace of God is present; the choice does not go away.

I want to address the topic of Judas. Here is the thing about Judas. If someone was going to betray Jesus, why

65 John 3:16
66 2 Thessalonians 3:2

did it have to be Judas? The reason it was Judas is that he had already made a choice about what he was going to do. Judas had set his worldview on trying to get things outside of God's timing. As a result, Judas was accustomed to acting according to what was in his heart.

When we talk about God watching our hearts, God watches both what we are thinking and how we are looking at things. God chooses us and puts us in the context of the decision He has already made, but it is still *our* choice. The way we structure our hearts allows God to do that. God simply would not use a righteous person to betray Jesus. We keep talking as though we can come up with something based on our sentiment. Are you saying that because God is a Father, He would not punish anybody or separate them? The very foundation of love is that if someone wants to be separated, you choose to let them go. It is not real love if you force a person into a relationship they do not want. The church really needs to deal with this issue. Are you going to remove John 3:16? Are you saying that everyone believes what the Bible says? Do you even believe that? And you wonder why young people are leaving the church. You are taking away their freedom by teaching them they do not have a choice in an age of freedom where everyone has unlimited choices. How exactly has that Gospel been working out for you?

The early church, which preached freedom, had more souls and converts than you do. The evangelists who tell people they have choices are the ones who win souls. If you are one who takes away the choices of those to whom you speak, you have likely not won any to Christ. By removing choice and free will from a person, you are taking away what it means to be human. Do you really believe that human beings do not want freedom just because God is omnipresent and omnipotent? Father God was the one who made the decision to give man the capacity for a free choice; it was not man who did that. Can you imagine God telling Adam and Eve, "There's a tree in the garden. I have given you a choice whether to eat from it or not, but I have already decided you will eat from it, whether you want to or not. And if you eat from it because I made you eat from it, I will punish you for eating from it, even though you did not have a choice." What kind of Gospel would that be? Yet some of you believe in that foolishness. It is foolishness because you are removing the principle of justice from the Gospel. By subscribing to that nonsense, you are saying that there is no justice. You are actually advocating that God owes an apology to everyone He has punished.

Responsibility is based on choice, and choice is based on freedom! Just because you are saved does not mean that everyone should be saved. You do not even know what you are advocating when you say such a thing. God intentionally chose to create human beings who could disobey Him, and now you want to be better than God and say that human beings do not have a choice? Let me be clear—salvation has been offered to everyone unequivocally, but every individual member of humanity must choose whether they want to spend eternity with God.

This is a good example: Oprah said that everyone is going to go to heaven. The issue with this doctrinal statement is that now you are taking away my freedom to hate God. You are forcing me into your heaven and your choice. What if I do not want to spend time with your God? Am I going to go to heaven even though I hate your God? I do not want to be there just because you think I should be.

The funny thing is that unbelievers understand choice and free will better than most of those who claim to be Christians. If you have not seen the show *Lucifer*, I encourage

you to watch it and see how unbelievers approach the devil.[67] You will find that many of them understand Scripture better than you do. For example, in one episode, Gabriel comes from heaven and speaks to Lucifer. Gabriel says, "Daddy really wants you back home." But Lucifer replies, "No, I hate Him. I'm not going back." You see, this response illustrates that the issue is not with God, but with the freedom He has given us.

It is important not to make it seem as though God's love is diminished if someone decides to reject Him. God's love is not affected by rejection; it may cause pain in His heart, but it is an eternal decision that whoever believes will have everlasting life. It is not right to twist Scripture and add your own personal beliefs to try to put limits on God. As a Jew, I would hate God for making us suffer, removing us from Israel, and putting us in Africa because the scattering has caused most African Jews to forget their heritage. Consequently, they must be taught their true identity and place in the tribe of Israel.

If you read the Hebrew Scriptures, it says that those who reject God will be cut off from the tribe of Israel forever.[68] This is because man is a sovereign being, and we tend to underestimate both the sovereignty of God and the sovereignty God has given to man. It is as if you are treating God as a court jester. You say we must follow His commands, but you also say that God might punish us if we do not follow them. If that was the case, I would be better off in Judaism because, at least in Judaism, I know I have a choice to follow God every day. When you say that I do not have a choice, you are taking away my humanity and making me less than what God created me to be. God does not have a problem with me rejecting Him, so why should you? The idea that everyone

67 https://en.wikipedia.org/wiki/Lucifer_(TV_series)
68 Jeremiah 31:36

must believe exactly what Europeans believe to be righteous is absolute nonsense.

The Scripture says,

> **But to all who did receive him, who believed in his name, he gave the right to become children of God...."[69]**

This verse is clearly referring to the freedom of choice given to man. Receiving the Lord Jesus Christ leads us to being trained as sons of God. Not everyone is a son, but Jesus still died for everyone. However, you are free to choose *not* to accept what is written. After all, Jesus even said to the Jews,

> **...Yet you refuse to come to me that you may have life[70]**

The Lord Jesus Christ even said that some of them were children of the devil. He said,

> **You are of your father the devil, and your will is to do your father's desires. He was a murderer from the beginning, and does not stand in the truth, because there is no truth in him. When he lies, he speaks out of his own character, for he is a liar and the father of lies.[71]**

You might think that you are greater than Jesus, but just remember, Jesus Himself said that some people are children of the devil. This is not the only verse in Scripture that mentions this, by the way. So what are we doing?

Does it hurt God's heart when people reject Him? Of course, it does! But God is not you. God's decisions are made in eternity, not in the boundaries of time. You are being trained to be like God, but you are not a god yet; there are

---

69 John 1:12
70 John 5:40
71 John 8:44

still things you do not understand. Stop acting as if you know everything about God. I do not. However, I do know what is written in Scripture. If you confront me, I will debate with you. I will not run away, and I certainly will not show mercy in the debate. I will show grace, but not mercy. I believe that this is a problem with many Christians. They want to throw out something and just walk away. You cannot do that with me; you cannot do that with any serious scholar either. In Judaism, we sit in fellowship, argue, and yet still leave the gathering in peace. Most Christians do not seem to know how to have a proper debate.

Christians need to relearn how to have constructive debates. For example, you should allow me to state my case without being so ready to say that you do not agree. What does that kind of response mean? It means nothing. Instead, train yourself to present the reasoning behind your stance in a thoughtful manner: one, two, three, four, five, etcetera. I have challenged people teaching specific subjects before in this way. I have said, "Show me what you are saying is in the original Greek. Show me where it is in the original Hebrew language." Christians need to stop quoting their King James Version.

It amazes me how many people who do not read the original language make all these doctrinal declarations. This is a serious issue. It is not in the Scripture; the Scripture ends with a separation. There is a clear separation of people who do not believe, but it is not based on God hating them. Free will and choice are based on God's love because to put someone in a context where they do not want to be is an act of hatred. If I took you now and put you where you are not supposed to be, you would hate it. Furthermore, for me to do such a thing would mean that I hate you and that I do not like you. I may want to change you, but it does not alter the

fact that you have not made the choice to be there. If I was taken to heaven and I did not want to be there, then it would be like a prison house for me.

Remember, the Bible balances God as merciful and God as judge. An unbeliever is an unbeliever. Someone who refuses to believe simply refuses to believe. Your faith cannot work for them, and your desire for them to be saved is not enough to overcome their choice to reject salvation. Every human being is a mystery because each one is a sovereign being. You cannot do anything to change them unless they decide from within themselves to change. God will not force them to change either. They have to come to their own choice, which must arise from inside of them.

The same reasoning holds true for you as well. If you had no choice about becoming a son, then you would still have behaved like a slave after becoming a son specifically because your sonship was not your choice. That is why you had to say, "Yes" when you became a Christian. Can anyone become a Christian without saying "Yes" to the Lord Jesus Christ? The answer is a hard no! You are not going to be born again by simply being inside a church. Your conscious and intentional choice to say, "Yes" to Jesus saved you. Your choice in that moment transformed you.

God gave you the capacity to make independent choices. Even knowing that you might choose a path that would cause you both pain, God still gave you the capacity to choose. Human free will and choice are real. God is not playing a game with human beings. I am with Einstein on this one: God does not play dice with the universe. God does not do "eeny, meany, miny, moe!"

Jesus Himself tells the parable of the goats going one way and the sheep going the other way.[72] How do you ignore so much of what Jesus said? So much of what is filling Christian social media right now is all about hell. The truth is that the church truly does not have a good doctrine on hell. And the reason that the church never really developed a proper doctrine of hell is because the church caused *everything* to become a hell. The fact is that there is more to it than what you have grown up thinking of as hell. Hell is both a living space *and* a living being. Allow me to push your boundaries a little here. The abyss is different from hell, and so is the lake of fire. These are three different things mentioned in the Scripture that the church never adequately explains.

If someone says there is no hell, they are not necessarily a heretic. The problem is that they are simply using the English word "hell." Hell is both a living entity and the dwelling place of Death. Death and hell are intertwined. Once Death and hell are removed, there is no more hell, but there is still a lake of fire and an abyss. This is clearly stated in the Scripture. The problem is that the church never fully developed this doctrine. They just warned people about going to hell. Furthermore, hell is not a permanent place. If hell were a permanent place, why would it be cast into the lake of fire?

Do you see why it is important for us to ask serious questions? As Christians, we must be willing to ask and answer the hard questions. If you are a Universalist, you say on the one hand that I do not have a choice, but then you want to judge me when I sin. You want to tell me I am wrong. You want to discipline me and you think I should be trained. But if I do not have a choice or my choice does not matter, what right do you have to tell me that I am doing something wrong? For that matter, why do you talk about right and wrong when you believe that there is no free choice? If there is no free choice, then there is no moral rightness or wrongness; nothing could ever really be wrong. Anything I do is okay because I do not have a free choice. According to that broken doctrine, I have no freedom; therefore, whatever I do must be accepted by you.

Such false doctrines, accompanied by the lack of development in the church's capacity for critical thinking, have serious implications for social relationships and the way we communicate and coexist with each other. If we do not address these issues, humanity could start engaging in ungodly behavior and easily justify it as acceptable. Did you know that this is exactly what the Masons believe? They believe that there is no distinction between good and evil, no objective morality. Therefore, they harm people because they believe that it is simply the way the world. Do you agree with that viewpoint? They may even go so far as to sacrifice an entire city. Following this doctrine can be very dangerous, not only for individuals but also for the social, economic, and political structures of the world.

Why did we judge the Nazis? Why do we, as Israelites and Jews, continually search for Nazis to stop them? If we say that there is no freedom, then what the Nazis did by orchestrating the holocaust would be deemed necessary and not sinful. If you subscribe to this false doctrine, it would mean that your God needs to apologize to all of us Jews and admit His wrongdoing by putting us through all of that pain and suffering. Make no mistake, we Jews suffered greatly and paid an incalculably heavy price.

I know that you will say that Jesus did not have a choice in going to the cross, but I disagree. You are going to say the Messiah did not have a choice because your theology says He did not. If you take that stance, you then have to ask what truly happened in the garden. Why did Jesus have to submit to the Father's will? You know that if Jesus had not submitted to God's will in the Garden of Gethsemane, He would not have died. He had to submit His will to the Father in order to die on the cross. The Lord Jesus Christ even says,

> **No one takes it from me, but I lay it down of my own accord. I have authority to lay it down, and I have authority to take it up again.[73]**

If Jesus made a conscious and willful choice, how can you think it is right to remove the capacity for choice from Christianity? And then there is that powerful phrase that preachers have always preached on in the book of Isaiah:

> **And I heard the voice of the Lord saying, "Whom shall I send, and who will go for us?"[74]**

Why ask this question if man does not have the freedom to choose?

Let me pose a couple of questions. Why would Paul make a point to mention his assistants who departed from his service? Why did Paul say they used to be a part of us, but they decided to leave?[75] Why should we believe in anything if we are not free to choose our belief? The whole concept of faith and belief is wasted if we do not have the freedom to choose. The real issue with this theology is the injustice of God when it comes to people who have suffered because they disobeyed. Your wishful thinking that everyone is already saved does not mean that God is unjust. It also does not mean that God is going around trying to kill or torment people.

---

73 John 10:8
74 Isaiah 6:8
75 2 Timothy 4:10

The reality is that our God has given us free will and the capacity to choose. Consequently, all we need to do is shout out to God, and He'll run to deliver us. If we refuse to look and repent, God will keep waiting. I do not believe God is going around trying to hug some people and kill others. I believe God has given us a choice and is just waiting for us to come to Him. Think about how long it took you to pray to be saved. I believe in the mercy of God. I believe that His mercy is quick and that the punishment of His anger lasts only for a moment. However, for His mercy to take effect, there must come a point where one accepts it. This is the Gospel of the Lord Jesus Christ. I travel the world spreading the Gospel and have won over 100,000 people to Christ through my crusades. How many souls have you won for Christ through your theology?

In fact, can you explain your theology? Are you simply talking about how many people come to know Christ because you preach the Gospel? Who is keeping count? I have been organizing crusades since I was a kid. Recently, I organized one for 30,000 people. Soon we will be holding a crusade for almost 70,000 people in seven villages in Africa where we will tell them they have a choice to choose Jesus or remain as they are. Am I lying when I tell them that they have a choice? If I am lying, then the consequences are greater for me since I am telling them they have a choice to choose God or not, when they do not actually have one. However, I have seen many things come and go since I began this work as a child. I saw the Jesus Movement, T.L. Osborne opening up Africa, and even witnessed miracles. James Swaggart went to South Africa, performing miracles, signs, and wonders, and people gave their lives to Christ. But now some Christian groups are not seeing any signs or wonders and are not winning anyone

to Christ. They have come up with a theology that says the world does not need to accept Jesus.

Let me be clear—the Lord Jesus Christ is still the *only* way. There is no other path to salvation. You have to choose Him. Before you think that I believe that when people who are not Christians die, that is the end, let me also clarify that I do not believe that.

In the book of Hebrews, it says:

...it is appointed unto man to die once, and after that comes judgment.[76]

That passage has nothing to do with you. In truth, it has everything to do with Christ! The whole passage deals with one death being the basis of judgment; it really has nothing to do with you. As such, a man's death is not the end of his possibility of knowing the Lord Jesus Christ.

We need to balance these things. I understand the desire to have people know the Lord, but I am not going to make God's word a lie just to achieve that. That is why I go out and win souls. What do you do? Sit down and have mystical experiences or argue over your experiences with some friends? Reaching souls is my job. I make altar calls even in my seminars in Africa and people come to Jesus. It is a work. I am not waiting for Jesus to appear to people as He appeared to me. Jesus gave me a task, and He gave you a task, too:

Go therefore and make disciples of all nations.[77]

Scripture does not say, "Go sit in the church."

76 Hebrews 9:27
77 Matthew 28:19

If you can do it physically, you should be able to leave your body and go to India to preach to a village. I have done that. So if you are doing this, you should be more powerful in winning souls. I am doing what I do because I have the ability and because I have the connections to allow me to travel throughout the world. It is important for us to love both our brethren *and* humanity. If you accept that as truth, then you need to stop saying that the human species is already saved. Instead, go get them to understand the Gospel that can actually save their lives. This is one of the greatest expressions of love. Go and convince them; bring them to the Gospel. The Gospel is still the Gospel; it has not changed. Somebody preached to you. Somebody witnessed to you and told you the first spiritual law. The first spiritual law is that it is appointed unto man to die because Jesus said so. From the moment you said, "Yes," you embarked on the journey to understanding the mysteries of who you are in your Father's kingdom. Despite having incorrect beliefs, you are still a child of God and learning how to function in your role as a son. Many people struggle to understand what it means to be a child of God and what their role is. It is easy to think that everyone is having the same spiritual experiences that you're having, but that is just not the case. Not everyone has said "Yes" to Jesus.

You are a child of God, and I wish the whole world would follow suit. However, there are those in the church who turn around and say that human beings have no freedom. This is something that worries me about this movement. Young people are not going to join something that takes away their freedom, especially in an age where freedom is so highly valued. Freedom is not a gift from Satan; it is a choice given to mankind by God! The only truly free being in the universe

is God, and out of His love, God gave freedom to those who believe in Him.

So if the Son sets you free, you will be free indeed.[78]

And if freedom is real, then

...where the Spirit of the Lord is, there is freedom.[79]

If someone tells you that there is no freedom, they are contradicting the Scriptures.

Did you know that there were Jews and Israelites who did not go with Moses, but instead preferred to stay in Egypt? They made a willful choice. While God may have chosen them, they did not choose God.

The reason I believe your Sonship is important is because, whatever God is, He has fully transferred into your being. You cannot talk about God being free and not accept that you are free yourself. You cannot talk about God being powerful and say that you are not a powerful being as well. You cannot talk about God being holy while saying that you are not holy yourself. By holiness, I do not mean the idea that you follow certain rules and consider yourself holy. The term "holiness" is a spatial term. It refers to something changing spaces or becoming a domain where something can be done.

People can determine their destiny in the context of a space. For example, there are at least four billion women on the face of the earth. I can look at those four billion women and choose one, bringing her into my space, making her holy in my space. The rest of them are not. Similarly, I can take a pen, one that belongs to someone else, and by taking it out of its original context and putting it into mine, it becomes holy

78 John 8:36
79 2 Corinthians 3:17

to me because I have changed the space. It is the context into which something or someone is placed that makes it holy, not its inherent nature. In Judaism, something can be unholy when it is outside the context of dedication, despite that it had been holy when it was dedicated. You are holy because of God. And because of God, you are now in a different space. You yourself have become a space where God can reside. Your holiness is a space precisely because you have changed spaces. Even though you do not always do things perfectly, God still considers you holy because holiness is not based on your activities. Again, it is a spatial concept. As long as you are dedicated to God and join yourself in the space of His divinity, your holiness remains.

The reason the Lord Jesus Christ became us, as stated in the book of Hebrews, is because salvation belongs to humanity, not to the angels. That is why angels are not subject to salvation, even though you may preach the salvation of Satan. The life of Jesus Christ is a reflection of who God wants to make us, as we were told by the early church fathers,

> **"For it was for this end that the Word of God was made man, and He who was the Son of God became the Son of man, that man, having been taken into the Word, and receiving the adoption, might become the son of God."[80]**

What He did not take into Himself is not subject to redemption and salvation. In other words, if you are not in Christ, you cannot be redeemed or become new. Paul says it this way:

> **Therefore, if anyone is in Christ, he is a new creation. The old has passed away; behold, the new has come.[81]**

---

80   Quote from St. Irenaeus of Lyons
81   2 Corinthians 5:17

This highlights the significance of our role in God's plan and the fact that we, and not the angels, are the recipients of salvation.[82] We are the ones who have the potential to become like God and to inherit the world to come, not the angels. Therefore, we must learn to take responsibility for who we are in God and understand the power that we have through our dedication to Him. God does not give help to the angels;[83] nor does He give them the world to come and subject it to them.[84] *You* are the ruler of the world to come, not the angels. The world to come belongs to you, not the angels. This is why you have to learn responsibility with who you are in God. What makes you powerful is that when you make a choice, God respects it.

So what does the frequency of Sonship mean for us? We cannot overstate its importance, as the Bible reminds us again and again. The fact that God made the son (Adam) and brought the woman out of the son (Adam) means that the woman has experienced being a son. In the first Adam, women had the experience of being sons.[85] It is in their DNA. It is easier for a woman to step back into Sonship than it is for a man to become a female. It is easier for a woman to step into Sonship because she originally came out of the son and experienced being a man when there was only one being. So, Eve experienced Sonship before she became a separate being.

Hebrews 6 says,

For it is impossible, in the case of those who have once been enlightened, who have tasted the heavenly gift, and have shared in the Holy Spirit, and have tasted the

---

82 Hebrews 1:5
83 Hebrews 2:16
84 Hebrews 2:5
85 In rabbinical literature the First Adam is called Adam HaRishon, meaning the first man was both male and female.

goodness of the word of God and the powers of the age to come, and then have fallen away, to restore them again to repentance, since they are crucifying once again the Son of God to their own harm and holding him up to contempt.[86]

Why would the Bible use the term "fallen away" if it was not possible? Scripture is not even talking about ordinary Christians here; it is talking about people who have experienced the age to come. That means they have already left this realm and visited what God is doing in the other realm. These people have been to that city; they have been to that realm. Most of you reading my words right now do not have the capacity to backslide. You have not earned that right. You are just upset. Think seriously about it, and while you are doing so, read the passage from Hebrews 6. Look at everything it talks about regarding the person who can actually backslide. That is why Peter's situation was not backsliding. Peter did not backslide.

So the question is, what is enlightenment? I would say it means to turn into light, to be illuminated, and to understand. Those who have illumination are not just those who understand in their heads, but they have actually experienced the reality of the light body. These people are not just in their heads. Rather, they have actually entered into light and their physical being has reflected that light. Have you ever had this experience in your life? If you think that your children have backslidden, let me tell you they have not. They are just angry with God and do not have enough experience to backslide. I am serious. That is why I do not consider young people as backsliders. Sometimes a young child may say, "I hate you", and sometimes they say, "I love you." The parents among you know how kids are. Once they turn 13 or 14 years old, they start saying things like, "I hate

---

86 Hebrews 6:4-6

you" and "You never let me do what I want to do." But that is not backsliding.

The writer of Hebrews says that all these concepts are elementary and pertain to eternal judgment:

Therefore let us leave the elementary doctrine of Christ and go on to maturity, not laying again a foundation of repentance from dead works and of faith toward God, and of instruction about washings the laying on of hands, the resurrection of the dead, and eternal judgment.[87]

Do you know what the heavenly gift that the writer of Hebrews is speaking of here? Let me surprise you—it is the gift of freedom. Do you know the power of freedom? I have a question for you, and this is not pride. Please forgive me if it sounds like it. How can you tell me that, according to the Bible, everyone is going to be saved? Do you realize that there are some people for whom you *should not* pray when they backslide?

You know, I have physically seen the Lord. I became a Christian through the appearance of Christ. I have actually been to heaven. I am not talking about going to heaven in my head. I have been physically transported. People have seen me in various places, and I knew I was there. Earlier this year, I sent someone to India who was invited to teach there. On a particular Sunday morning, they were teaching in church while we were in worship at home. I decided to enter into the service, and two of the guys who were there saw me so I had to step back.

Jesus has appeared to me in several different ways, including as a white man. This was difficult for me to accept because I hated the idea that white people had taken Jesus

87 Hebrews 6:1-2

and made Him in their image. They wanted the whole world to worship that image of the white Jesus. I regarded this as white people wanting to essentially be worshipped as God. They did not allow other cultures to have Jesus in their own likeness.

Despite my initial reservations, Jesus appeared to me in my study as a white person repeatedly. This was an interesting experience for me. As a black Jew, I did not meet a white Jew until much later in life. So when I became a Christian, my mental image of Moses was black, as was my image of Jesus. But the more I learned about history, the more I hated the idea of a white Jesus. I know that many black people feel the same way. For me as a Jewish black man, it was even more complicated.

White people would often ask me, "How can you be both Jewish and black?" And I would ask white Jews, "How can you be both white and Jewish?" This is a conversation that we, as Israelites, have constantly because we have been scattered all over the world. It is amusing to me that people think of Africa as though it was not part of the wider world when in fact the Jews were scattered all over the planet. The Lord said He would scatter the Jewish people to every nation on the earth,[88] but in the mind of most Europeans, Africa is not part of that earth. They think of the earth as if it was restricted to Europe. I was so opposed to the idea of a white Jesus that I almost started looking for a new name for the Messiah!

My mother is white and the woman who raised me is white. This is the irony of the whole situation. My children call my mother their grandmother. To give you an idea of how contradictory this is, and before you think I hate white people, my father-in-law and sons-in-law are all white. I just

88 Leviticus 26:33

do not want to have a white Jesus. A white mother and white father—that is. White sons-in-law? Sure. But a white Jesus? No! I was angry.

I know some of you will never admit to being racist because there was no racism born in you. I like it when people say that. But I was in my study, and I had been seeing Jesus as black all my life when this white Jesus showed up. It is not funny because I was in that basement drawing cosmic paintings. I was in the process of taking passages from the Bible, breaking them down on the walls, writing them on the floor in Hebrew, Greek, and ancient Aramaic, and putting them all together to try to figure out what the Scriptures meant. Jesus used to come in and talk to me as I was working. One day, He said, "This is what you must do." Every time I sat in my study, He would come in, sit by the table, and start asking me questions. My wife said that when she saw the movie *A Beautiful Mind*, it was exactly what I was doing in the basement.

We had angels bumping into people in our house. A friend from Nigeria came to our house once and was lying down on the bed. An angel came to look at him and he got scared; he even started binding the angel in the name of Jesus. I told him not to do that and he asked why. I remember saying, "Because if it is an angel of God, it will leave. Your theology is wrong because every angel is required to obey you if you ask them to leave in the name of Jesus. They cannot disobey you if you command them to leave in the name of Jesus." Unfortunately, some of you have chased away good angels out of fear in the name of casting out demons. Scripture says that every knee shall bow and every tongue shall confess.[89] This is referring not only to good angels or bad angels, but literally *every knee*. Even a good angel, when you command

---

89 Isaiah 45:23, Romans 14:11, Philippians 2:10

them to leave in the name of Jesus, must obey that command. That is why you should always ask who they are.

Let me return to the story of the white Jesus appearing in my study. When Jesus entered, I would not talk to him for a week. I asked the white Jesus, "Where do you keep my Jesus? You are not my Jesus!"

Jesus replied, "You are a racist."

I replied, "I am not a racist. I just do not want a white Jesus."

He retorted, "You are a racist, son."

I repeated, "No, I am not a racist." I then proceeded to ignore Him every day He came into my study. Until one day, the Lord sat down beside me and looked at me as I wept. I asked, "Why don't you give me my Jesus?"

The Lord responded, "You are a racist. Get your act together."

He continued to do this until one day, I said, "Okay, you are the Lord."

I talked to Jesus and asked, "Why did you do that, Jesus?" He did not stop. The next time, He came as a Chinese Jesus. I was so confused. I could understand a black or white Jesus, but a Chinese Jesus? I was angry and upset. I just wanted to see a Jewish guy with curly hair, even if He was white. But He kept saying, "Son, you are a racist."

I said, "I am not a racist. My mom is white, my dad who adopted me and brought me to Canada is white, and my brother, a lieutenant colonel in the US Army, is white."

The Lord responded, "You are racist, son. You are very racist."

I was angry, but I knew I had to listen to Him to learn. He continued to ignore me. He then came to me as an Indian (not an American Indian) and then as a Native American. Finally, Jesus came back as a black man and said, "I cannot help you until you deal with this issue."

It was only because this happened to me that I am now able to speak to people from all walks of life. You see, we often miss what God is trying to do in our lives. He wants to train us and bring us into Sonship. Most of us have not seen ourselves because we live in a politically correct society. If we were to appear in another culture, it would be seen as a cultural imposition. But God wants us to understand and embrace diversity. And that is exactly what God did! God became a human being. Jesus, when He resurrected, went to many different places in the world. I know Jesus was not white when He became a man, but how did white people decide to make Him white unless they had first seen Him as white? How did all the people in the world get to encounter him? You have to see Jesus the way He appears to you. Jesus has appeared to me like that for over 25 years now. He has taken me into different realms, but I am not allowed to talk about it. Now I am teaching things I knew 25 years ago.

The things I teach about the bride of Christ? I preached the same things 20 years ago, and people got very upset. The Lord said, "Shut up, son. It is not time yet." But I knew it was wrong even then. It is no surprise that most men are uncomfortable with a teaching that says they are brides!

Men will not tell you that they are uncomfortable with that. They say, "No, I do not want to be a wife." We forget that this is a very serious issue. If you have an experience like I or some other people have had, what kind of prayer are you going to pray for me? What would you say to me that is greater than the appearance of Jesus? If I denied Jesus tomorrow, what would you do? That is the point. The reason I have not returned to Judaism, especially given the foolishness of people in the church, is that I have seen Jesus. It would be impossible for me to do that and come back because I would have crucified Christ a second time.

By the way, this is exactly what John was writing about when he said, "Do not pray for them."[90] I do not mean that you should not pray for humanity. Nothing ever will change if all you are doing is sitting in your house and praying for Satan to repent. I keep asking those Christians who are teaching this nonsense, "Have you prayed for all the humans around you? Is that why the satanic is now your concern? Why are you trying to save demons when human beings are around you?" Foolishness! Their children are not safe, but they are busy trying to save demons. These people are trying to go to alien ships and save aliens, but their children do not know the Lord Jesus Christ.

It may sound simple, but here is the powerful thing about being a Son. When you are a Son, anything that God can become, you can become. God has made you in such a way that you carry that divine DNA within you. You are fully divine. Your Father did not make you and leave one limb of Himself outside of you. God did not put one foot into you and say, "Well, when you get better, I will put in the rest." He is your Father in heaven. God does not know how to do things halfway. God is not going to come partially into your life. The Lord has chosen to be *completely* present in you so that everything He has is in you. Even right now, while you as a son are sitting and reading this book, you can create a

90   1 John 5:16-17

world. You are probably thinking that it is not possible. I ask, "Why not?"

Do not get me wrong though—this idea scares me. The idea that God has actually stepped into me, allowing me access to the fullness of who He is inside this body is scary. You walk around in this world appearing normal, yet you are not actually normal. It may sound harsh to say it that way, but it is true. Paul himself said that we are not mere men.[91] You are not a mere mortal human being. You are not just a man. I tell you, you are an embodiment of Divinity walking upon the earth. If God were to unleash that full potential within you as you are now, you would destroy the world because of your divine nature. God is holding it back. It is not you holding it back; God is protecting the world from you until you reach maturity.

Your soul, which came from heaven, is still developing. It is like a baby. The soul you have now is not the same soul with which you were born. You are a new creature with a new soul that needs to grow up so you can serve as a true channel for the full manifestation of Divinity. You are a child of God, born of the Spirit, with God having chosen to birth Himself into you. However, you were also given a new soul because a human cannot exist without one.

Your spirit is not a newborn baby because your spirit is God and it is ancient. What is the newborn baby that Paul talks about? A newborn baby desires milk. Your soul came into you without a record of sin. Your soul, which you are carrying now as a son of God and as a child of God, was born from above and does not have a record of anything that you did before you said "Yes" to Jesus. There is no record of sin in your soul. Otherwise, you would still be going the wrong way; you would still be a sinner. You would still be, fallen in

Adam. You are no longer fallen and there is power in your soul's purity. It is amazing! Two things are happening to you. God Himself has become the spirit inside you, and you received a new soul from heaven. The soul must be present. The soul you have now has come directly from heaven. It is not born from your body and it is not born from the earth. Your soul is no longer earthly in nature. Your new soul is now spiritual because it has entwined with the spirit, not with the body.

When I first became a Christian, I did not know what Christian doctrine was. I wanted to understand what Christianity was all about, but most people could not give me a clear answer. They just gave me their own opinions. However, it is important to remember that Christianity is not based on personal opinions. It is a well-defined system. Yes, the Holy Spirit moves, but for those of you who believe that doctrine is not important, consider this: Jesus died for a doctrine. If Jesus had answered, "No" when the Jews asked Him if He was the Son of God, He would not have been killed. This doctrine led to the death of the Lord Jesus Christ.

In John 10, the Jews tried to stone Him for this. Jesus asked why they were trying to stone him since He had done many good works. The Jews replied that it was not for His good works, but because He had claimed to be the Son of God.[92] In other words, they wanted to kill Jesus for a doctrine, not for His miracles, signs, wonders, or even His moral character. So before you think that doctrine is not important, remember Jesus and think again.

Furthermore, this doctrine was written on a sign that was placed over His head during Jesus' crucifixion.[93] The Jews asked Jesus to state His doctrine, which was, "Jesus Christ,

92 John 10: 31-39
93 John 19:19

King of the Jews." It is a doctrine. It is surprising to hear people say that Christianity is not about doctrine.

Finally, it is important to note that if someone dies for their faith in the Lord Jesus Christ, all of their moral failures are erased at the moment of their martyrdom. The reason why that works is that the gift of your life is greater than your moral character. So if the day comes that someone comes to you and asks if you believe in Jesus Christ, the Son of God and you say, "No" in order to escape death, you have failed. This is why the early church trained people to withstand persecution. The major question was not whether you were a moral person, or even a nice person, but whether you believed.

Remember Polycarp,[94] the disciple of John, who was respected and loved in his city? They asked him to pretend to light the idol and renounce Jesus without saying it. But Polycarp said, "I have served him for 80 years and He has never forsaken me. Why must I forsake him now?" Then Polycarp was set on fire and died for his faith in the Lord Jesus Christ.

Many Christians claim to be moral, but when it comes time to actually make a sacrifice, to believe and put their lives on the line, they are not willing to do so. Martyrdom is a real thing; it takes away everything. A person's morality does not really matter when they give their life for Christ. If you go to places where Christians are being killed, you will understand the tangible strength of belief intrinsic to those people who truly believe in Christ and are willing to die for their faith. It is surprising how people who claim to

94 https://en.wikipedia.org/wiki/Polycarp

be moral are the ones who quickly deny Jesus and run away. It is a strange thing.

It is easy to talk about Christ and engage in meaningless arguments when there is no persecution. But let the Muslims come to burn your church in Nigeria and we will see how your doctrine holds up. This is a serious topic. We talk about these women who gave their lives for Christ. They did it because they looked at the life of the Lord Jesus Christ and realized that, if God was making them the same as Christ, then they must be willing to go through what Jesus did in order to live their lives for the salvation of others. Every nation on earth has sacrificed Christians to become a Christian nation. Europeans tend to forget how many Christians they killed before they became Christian. For example, in Armenia, Bartholomew was skinned alive. The Armenians laid his skin on his hand and he died. Fifty years later, the whole nation converted.

Being a mystic will not protect you from persecution. I used to think that if I went to heaven, I could just stay there and no one would persecute me. However, following Jesus requires you to be willing to lay down your life. God knows that your life might be the foundation of a new world. You may not want to hear this, but you are going to rule worlds. If God is going to put you over worlds, then you must be willing to give up your divinity for the world. It is not about being a god; it is about being willing to give up your godhood so that others can be saved.

In Sonship, you need to be able to do kenosis,[95] which means to empty yourself of all power and subject yourself to something to which you should not have to subject yourself. You are following Jesus, are you not? You are not following me; you are following God. Sonship means that there are

95 https://en.wikipedia.org/wiki/Kenosis

worlds within you. You carry the seed of worlds because you are the foundation of the worlds. The Bible says that you are the righteousness of God and a foundation of worlds,[96] and you carry the seeds of those worlds within you.

The time will come when worlds will come out of your body. I have studied what the human body means to God. If you do not understand your body's value to the Father, you are missing something. Your body was not meant to die and God never created it to do so. It dies only because of sin and the curse that God placed on man. God tells Adam and Eve,

"...but of the tree of the knowledge of good and evil you shall not eat, for in the day that you eat of it you shall surely die."[97]

"The literal translation of this passage is, "In the day you eat, you will begin to die, you will keep on dying, you will continue to die, and you will die until you die." Let us quote the Hebrew again: מוֹת תָּמוּת (Mot Tamot). This curse was activated when Adam sinned and allowed death to enter into the world. The human will brought death into the world.

Before Adam sinned, death was not a part of creation. The human will activated death and made it a reality. Paul says,

Therefore, just as sin came into the world through one man, and death through sin, and so death spread to all men because all sinned....[98]

All of this was only potential until the human will activated it. When Eve ate from the tree, she was the one who started dying, not Adam. Death was not active in the universe, even as Eve began to deteriorate. She started to lose the glory,

96   Proverbs 10:25
97   Genesis 2:17
98   Romans 5:12

but death was not in the world yet. Remember, Eve was created from Adam. She was deteriorating, but it was not death yet. Death was still outside of creation. This changed the moment Adam ate the fruit because he did so by choice. (This is another verse for those who argue for Universalism, as it shows that man has the freedom to make choices.) Adam made the decision to side with his wife even though he knew the consequences of his actions. Adam chose to eat the fruit after looking into the future and knowing what was going to happen. It is important to note that Adam was the son of God and his decision was deliberate.

It is better to side with man when there is a problem rather than with God. This statement may come as a surprise to some since many people might think it is better to side with God. However, we must remember that God does not need our help. This is precisely why God punished Job's friends. They sided with God against Job, as demonstrated in Job 16 where Job says that a man who is suffering should be shown mercy by his friends, even if he forsakes the love of God.[99]

Their theology was sound, and everything they said about God was true. God was just and God was good. However, the attack on Job by siding with God was detested by God, precisely because God did not need their help. What their friend Job needed was their help. That is what it means to be a son.

Being a son means siding with those who cannot help themselves, just as Jesus did for us. Jesus did not defend God. Instead, He sided with us in our iniquity and sin. The Lord Jesus Christ chose to die for us rather than stay in heaven and enjoy forever what He was meant to do. This is what Adam did, which is why God made the promise He made to the woman, and why Adam was given a second chance.

99   Job 16:4,5,21

Adam chose to side with someone he knew God was going to destroy, giving his life to join his wife in death. Adam chose to leave heaven and depart from the garden, and though he later had buyer's remorse, his first decision was a good one. Adam made that decision as a son; he made the decision made in obedience to God. God brought sin into the world and it is man who must bear the sin.

You will never find a female sacrifice for the removal of sin. It is always male, be it the goat, the sheep, or the bull. That is because the male is the one who carries the seed of rebellion. As a son, you are represented by Melchizedek, the one who embodies what it means to be a son before you were even created. Through Melchizedek we observed the meaning of the sacrifice of the Lamb. It allows you to see the meaning and purpose of being a son before the world was created.

The same can be seen in the Garden of Eden, where the son Adam chose to be on the side of rebellion. In doing so, he laid down his life for his wife. Therefore, Sonship is intrinsic, sustains the universe, and brings redemption to it. By being a son, you are a redeemer and the manifestation of God's creative power. A son is the instrument of God's creative will. All of heaven was poured into you when you were born from heaven, making you the carrier of every intent of God.

This is precisely why sonship is an issue of fracticalization.[100] Those of you who are scientists understand what I mean when I say that a fractal is a piece of matter that contains the whole. As a son, you are a complete embodiment of Divinity, just as I am. Sonship is the piece of matter that contains God completely. If you examine every piece of matter, the fullness of the image is present within it.

100 https://atas.net/market-theory/fractality-what-the-principle-of-fractality-is/

You and I both carry this image. We also hold the depths of Divinity within us. So, anything we do in life or death carries the intent of God within it. When we fell, the entire universe followed us. I have given many teachings on how man was created. Shortly put, the idea is that as a son, you carry worlds within you. The universe itself pays close attention to your thoughts, words, and actions. The universe is your cosmic "Big Brother," if you will, even if you are not aware of it. The implication of this truth is that much of what happens in the world could easily be a result of the way Christians think. God does not really care about the thoughts of unbelievers. However, He does care about *your* thoughts. Why does God care? He cares because you carry His divine nature. As long as you and I do not understand our Sonship, the world will keep doing what it is doing.

Do you realize that the complete understanding of your divine Sonship is a big part of God's goal? Coming to an understanding of who you are is a key to the healing of the world. This is what we call in Hebrew "Tikkun Olam,"[101] which means the repairing of the world. The world is repaired through the manifestation of Sonship. God pays attention to what you think. We quote the following passage all the time:

"For as he thinks in his heart, so is he."[102]

Because of your Sonship, your thoughts frame the world. It is amazing that, since we started thinking about immortality, scientists have started exploring how to create and extend human longevity. That really only started once it became a major talking point in the church. It is the same as when the church started talking about healing. When spiritual people

---

101 https://en.wikipedia.org/wiki/Tikkun_olam
https://www.chabad.org/library/article_cdo/aid/3700273/jewish/What-Is-Tikkun-Olam.htm

102 Proverbs 23:7 (NKJV)

seriously think about things, the universe responds to them. Otherwise, why would God tell you to watch what you think? Do you think the Lord tells you to watch what you think because He might not like it? No. It is because the frequency of Sonship that you carry travels through your thoughts and impacts the foundation of the universe. You will be surprised at what happens in your environment when you change the way you think.

Look at Adam as a son who was created and formed by God. Sonship that is created is not the same as Sonship by birth. I make a distinction between the two because the created son fell. The born Son, however, has not fallen. I use the word "has" deliberately because you also are a son born from heaven and have not fallen. You did not fall. You descended. These are two very different things; a descent is not a fall. The first Adam, who was a son of creation, fell. Adam fell below his creation status, creating a barrier that he could not transcend. He was a son, but Adam was not like God. He had the capacity for creativity, but Adam did not have a spirit. I know you may be confused, but where does it say in the Bible that Adam had a spirit? It does not. Scripture says that Adam had a living soul. If you look closely at the passage, the first Adam was of the earth. He was earthly by nature.[103] That means that the first Adam was twice a person of earth. In 1 Corinthians 15, it says the first man was of the earth. Adam was earthly, twice earthly since Adam's soul was from earth, not from heaven. God interacted with Adam's earthly body. This interaction between the body and God produced the soul. The soul you had before you became a believer was the production of God and your earthly body.[104]

The Bible states that Adam was made a living soul. In Genesis 2, God breathed (Hebrew: wayyippah) into him and

103 1 Corinthians 15:47
104 Genesis 2:7

he became a nephesh chayyah,[105] or a living soul, not a living spirit. This is a concept that many find hard to believe, let alone understand, despite the clear wording in the Scripture. However, it is a very important distinction.

I understand what you are probably thinking: "Who knows if the spirit of man rises or descends?"[106] Solomon asked this same question, but it is not an answer. Yet many Christians turn this verse into a statement instead of recognizing it as the question that it was. The word used here is "breath."[107] Just because something breathes does not mean it has a spirit, let alone a soul. Otherwise, a tree would have a spirit and that could easily lead to a belief in animism—not a good thing.

A plant is said to have a soul because it breathes, and that which breathes is alive. Your clothes may also be considered to have a soul, as they breathe as well. Every fabric maker knows that cloth must allow air to circulate in order to be comfortable to wear. Cotton, for example, breathes and is considered alive even though it may appear to be dead.

One reason priests wear linen and other traditional material is because they are considered alive. There are certain things that Jews are told not to wear, not because they are bad, but because they are not considered alive. People may not like to think about it, but it is quite reasonable that these materials breathe. Every priest must wear garments of living materials because the priest is a symbol of life within the community. On a side note, you should remember that just because someone breathes does not necessarily mean that they are alive. The Bible states that Adam was a living soul, not a living spirit. When Adam disobeyed God, he died. In that moment, Adam went from being a living soul

---

105 wayyippah וַיִּפַּח nephesh וַיִּפַּח chayyah חַיָּה
106 Ecclesiastes 3:26
107 rū·ah חוּר

to existing as a dead soul. The Bible also says that you were dead in your trespasses,[108] referring to the time before you accepted Jesus Christ as your savior.

Paul talks about the Lord Jesus Christ as the second man.[109] Jesus is YHVH from heaven. The second man is the Lord from heaven. Paul says that the second man was a life-giving spirit. The Principle of Sonship means that the true Son is a life-giving being. Even Adam, being a living soul, was a life-giving being. When Adam died, his soul produced only dead souls filled with sin because of Adam's dead state. On the other hand, the new Adam, the Lord Jesus Christ, is a life-giving spirit.

Do you remember what I said before about the lamb that was slain before the foundation of the world? When God spoke, life flowed from Him. God's speech distilled itself accordingly and framed the Word. That Word takes on the form it needs to be. If it needs to be a butterfly, the Word becomes a butterfly. If it is a worm, the Word becomes a worm. The same Word produces all things while the distillation process is the Son. The Son is the filter through which the fractalizing light of creation passes to frame everything. Even Adam, when he was a living soul, could do all kinds of things in creation. You might think that God made the trees, but you would be mistaken. God did not make trees; God made seeds. Read your Bible—Adam made the trees.

Let me give you another example. When God created the animals, they were not here on the earth. They were in another realm, as clearly stated in Genesis 1. The trees of the field were not present on the earth either, because there was no man to till the ground.[110] Adam had not yet been created.

108 Colossians 2:13
109 1 Corinthians 15:47
110 Genesis 2:5

Until the son was present on earth, God's creation could not manifest. When the son arrived, creation was released. The moment Adam was created, the rain started to fall, providing the necessary moisture for seed to grow upon the face of the earth. It was the presence of the son in the world which caused the rain to come down. When the son fell, everything else followed and became smaller in scale.

The Bible says that God made all the great things; so let me ask you, how did God make the animals pass before Adam? What does it mean to name something? When you name something, you are giving it a destiny and a way of acting. Adam named the elephant and gave it its function. God created it in the beginning; however, its form on earth was from the mouth of Adam. Whatever Adam named something, that is what it was called. In the West, naming does not mean much, yet in most other cultures, the act of naming gives something its destiny and purpose.

Who gives purpose to creation—Adam or the son? Whose voice speaks and creation listens because God gave them authority? You! This does not mean that God does not have power. Christians really need to accept that God is not afraid to share His power. God gives His power to those He trusts— the sons. According to Jewish teachings, Adam could go everywhere in the universe. Adam could go to other galaxies, even visit other universes. So can you.

God planted the garden to show His son what to do. He did not plant everything everywhere because He wanted to provide an example for the son to follow in the world. God created more than 90% of the world, but there was little growth in it because a son was going to be born and be given the capacity to replicate what God was doing everywhere else in the universe. However, the son fell and rendered himself unable to fulfill this purpose. As a result, the universe God created remained as it was. God is a God of demonstration; He wanted to show the son how to create. The garden was a way for the son to learn and understand the creative process. It is important that we understand the purpose behind God's actions in creating the world and the role that the son was intended to play. In Genesis 2, we know that God rested from all of His works. However, this is not what the Hebrew text or the rabbis' interpretation says. It states that God rested from all the works He had created to be done.[111] This means that God stopped because He had created work for you to complete. That is why the only thing described in the text is a garden. You are responsible for finishing the work.

That is right—you are responsible for bringing other planets to life. Your DNA must be transferred to these planets, even in your natural life. After the first Adam failed, the second Adam, Jesus Christ, came into the world to restore both the concept of Sonship and the ability to bring forth life in every dimension. The first Adam had the potential to do so, but he failed. The Sonship you now carry is not just a soul-based one, but a spirit-based one. This means that your Sonship allows you to participate in the descent of YHVH. The second Adam, Jesus Christ, is the YHVH from heaven and was made a life-giving spirit.

Your Sonship differs from that of Adam because your Sonship is the descent of God into human form. Think about it like this: in whatever way Scripture describes the Lord Jesus Christ, the Bible is also describing you. Do not remove yourself from it. Those who are born from above are sons. The second frequency is the Frequency of Sonship and it is a frequency greater than the universe. The Frequency of Sonship is the frequency of the interior resonance of Divinity, meaning your sound is inside of God. That is what it means to be a son. Your sound is the same as the sound inside of God.

111 Genesis 2:2: The Hebrew word used here is from Asah, to make, to do.

The resonance you carry *is* the divine resonance. Creation itself knows you!

To put it another way, creation is not the problem; you are. You simply do not know who you are. Even if as you are reading this, you are telling yourself you do not believe my words, your unique sound is vibrating within God because you are a son. God does not want to be known any other way except through you. This is the choice God made. He does not want to be known through angels. He does not want to be known by the animals. He does not want to be known through the trees or the flowers. He does not want to be known through the mountains, hills, rivers, or even the Seraphs. God only desires to be known through the son, and *you* are that son.

It is precisely because God wants to be known through you that He chose to become you, to become man. God did not become an angel. Angels do not carry the DNA of God. You do. Angels do not resonate within Divinity. You do. Angels do not carry the full intent of God for creation. You do. You are far more marvelous than you think, and evermore amazing than you have yet to grasp. You are the only way God wants to experience the world. God has chosen you as the vessel of His experience of the world that He created. You are the Terminus Ad Quem of Divinity.[112] You are the edge of divine consciousness. When God wants to experience anything in the world, He does so through you because you are a son. How would your life change if you really believed and understood just how much your experiences matter to God? Consider this for a moment. Because of your unique nature as a son, when you touch something, God is experiencing matter in a way that He could not before because God has never been a material being. Everything you touch sends an

112 Terminus Ad Quem: goal, object, or course of action: destination, purpose. https://www.merriam-webster.com/dictionary/terminus%20ad%20quem

experience of the world that God created back into Him from the perspective of a human son. Your materiality is vitally important to God. God does not have a problem with this because you are His son. He *wants* to experience the world through you. Remember, God had never died until He became human, experiencing death *as* a human. God had never gone hungry until He became human and experienced hunger as a man.

Some of you may argue that Jesus never sinned, but Jesus was tempted to sin in all kinds of ways. God had never been tempted until He took on a human body. Only then did God get to experience the fullness of what it means to be human. For this very reason, after God experienced the world through a human body, His relationship with us changed. It is through Sonship that God's relationship with the world changed. The world was created and saved, and the mind of God was restructured in relationship to both us and creation through Sonship. Sonship is the frequency of the experience of God, the frequency with which the world was created to engage. God does not want to experience the world anywhere else except through His sons.

Sonship is everything!

Chapter 4

THE FREQUENCY
OF KINGSHIP

I am shocked at how many Christians pass by beggars on the street without giving them anything. Why do you drive by without giving them the spare change in your car? Do you understand what you are doing? Most of that money might well end up getting lost, but are you really so destitute that you cannot spare a few coins to help someone in need? How can you talk about being in the line of Melchizedek when you fail to show compassion? Where is your love? It is important for us to remember this. Most of that change in your car will probably get lost, and realistically will not have very much of an impact on your monthly electric bill, so why not give a little bit of that pocket change to another human being? We need to be honest with ourselves and our thoughts. We often think that the person begging is lying about their situation, or that they will use the money for drugs.

But ask yourself this: why does that matter? Shouldn't that be a reason for us to be even more compassionate?

This is about a cosmic principle. Every day, with every action, you are practicing your role as ruler of the world, transforming and repairing it. It is a big deal. You are exercising your divinity. Becoming a god is easy; it is not complicated. God exposes Himself to the world, making Himself accessible like water for a hedgehog to drink. To be like God, you must become a sacrament for the universe. If you want to emulate your Father, then you must do so. We must cultivate this mindset in every aspect of our lives. This disposition towards humanity reconfigures our psychology and sets us apart from general society. We treat *all* people as human beings and not constantly judge them. It actually requires less effort to withhold judgment than it does to judge everything as you have probably been doing. You know that someone who writes about judging others is probably a person whose entire life has been spent searching for a platform and seeking personal gain. They cannot attain it, so they lash out at others.

This leads me to this principle of trading. I did not come up with the trading doctrine, but I believe I must defend someone who has helped so many people. Some may misuse the teachings, but that is not the fault of the person who introduced trading to us. I believe the teaching on giving and trading is one of the greatest teachings to come into the body of believers. Even churches are embracing it, not forcing people to give. It is amazing to see what is happening.

We do not focus on giving and I rarely take offerings. My wife has to remind me to do so. People are trading and giving and, as a result, people are receiving help. Those in need are being taken care of. This is because people are trading their finances. When I have visitors come to my home, I do not expect them to spend their own money to feed themselves. If I invite you for a visit and you stay for a month, I will make sure you are fed. I hope you see my point now. The issue is how God created the world. God is a substance and He transfers His substance. God sends rain and His Son, both of which are manifestations of His substance. It is the divine substance of God that sustains both the wicked and the righteous, feeding the sinners and the saints. And what is the amazing part? God never asks if a person is a sinner before providing for them.

Are you starting to understand what being divine truly means? It does not mean that you sit in judgment over everyone with the power to help them. The Bible does not say anywhere that you should give up everything, except for the case of the rich young ruler. The teaching of the Bible is that you should always give from your surplus. This is a very serious matter. If you say that you do not have a surplus, this means you are saying that God has not blessed you. You are claiming that you do not waste money, that you use all the money you have. That is just not true. We practice trading because it is important for your spiritual enlightenment. Trading with the poor person who asks you on the street is important for the universe.

It is amazing that God gives you all this power, and He does not ask you to change the world. Yes, you are capable of doing so; yet, all God asks is for you to take care of the guy on the street corner. He knows that guy represents the world. What if the 25 cents you gave to that person could repair the world, not because of the amount, but because of who gave it. You are the one doing it. Study the book of Hebrews and you will see this principle laid out clearly.

The first frequency of Melchizedek is the Frequency of Sacrifice, and it is foundational. The second is the Frequency of Sonship, an intrinsically and internal divine principle. The Frequency of Sonship is embedded in everything. If you are a Son, then you are everything that God is. Even your mind is the mind of God.

Notice that I said, "...the mind of God." I know Paul said, "...the mind of Christ." I am doing this deliberately because I believe that the Lord Jesus Christ *is* God. If you are a son, then you are a carrier of the mind of God; you are operating on what I call the "edge of divine consciousness." This means that nothing happens in creation without first passing through you. If it is happening, it is because some believer somewhere allowed it to happen. Some son of God let it happen. It is in the Bible. The passage, "we have the mind of Christ," is clearly all about the mind.

> **For who knows a person's thoughts except the spirit of that person, which is in him? So also no one comprehends the thoughts of God except the Spirit of God. Now we have received not the spirit of the world, but the Spirit who is from God, that we might understand the things freely given us by God. And we impart this in words not taught by human wisdom but taught by the Spirit, interpreting spiritual truths to those who are spiritual.**

> **The natural person does not accept the things of the Spirit of God, for they are folly to him, and he is not able to understand them because they are spiritually discerned. The spiritual person judges all things, but is himself to be judged by no one. "For who has understood the mind of the Lord so as to instruct him?" But we have the mind of Christ.[113]**

It says, "... who knows a person's thoughts except the spirit of that person, which is in him?" Paul is not talking about

---

113 1 Corinthians 2:11-16

spirit here; he is talking about the mind. When you are a son, you stand at the edge of divine consciousness, meaning you can look directly into the mind of God.

This is a Melchizedek Principle because Melchizedek is a witness to God becoming a Lamb. Melchizedek also accepted the responsibility of sacrificing the Lamb so that a world could come into being. You have the mind of Christ, which is the mind of God. If Christ is God, then it does not matter how many ways you slice it. It is as Paul says, "You have the mind of God."

Understanding the nature of the mind of Christ is important. God creates the universe *through the mind of Christ*. When the Greeks refer to Jesus Christ as the Nous,[114] it is equivalent to referring to Jesus as the Logos.[115] It is interesting that the phrase says, "You have that mind." A son is the carrier of the Logos principle. I did not say Rhema; I said Logos. I know many of you reading this book come from a Pentecostal background and you might say, "I do not want the Logos; I want the Rhema."[116] If you have ever made that statement, then I have some bad news for you. What you

---

114 https://Biblehub.com/greek/3563.htm
   noús (a masculine noun) – the God-given capacity of each person to think (reason); the mind; mental capacity to exercise reflective thinking.

115 https://Biblehub.com/greek/3056.htm
   III. In several passages in the writings of John ὁ λόγος denotes the essential Word of God, i. e. the personal (hypostatic) wisdom and power in union with God, his minister in the creation and government of the universe, the cause of all the world›s life both physical and ethical, which for the procurement of man›s salvation put on human nature in the person of Jesus the Messiah and shone forth conspicuously from his words and deeds.

116 https://Biblehub.com/greek/4487.htm
   a spoken word, made «by the living voice" is commonly used in the NT (and in LXX) for the Lord speaking His dynamic, living word in a believer to inbirth faith

have effectively just said is, "I do not want Jesus; I want my own Word." Look at what the Bible says:

> **In the beginning was the Word [Logos], and the Word [Logos] was with God, and the Word [Logos] was God. He was in the beginning with God. All things were made through him, and without him was not anything made that was made.**[117]

It was not the Rhema!

There is not one mention of Rhema in John Chapter 1. God bless our father, Kenneth Hagin,[118] but his teaching on this matter was in error. Effectively, he taught the whole body of Christ to say that they do not want Jesus. The repercussions of that error are still felt all throughout Pentecostalism. Nobody had the nerve to challenge him back then, or it would have been corrected. But the fact of the matter is a son is a Logos-centric principle.

Logos is that which frames the structure, the foundation of anything. You are not just a new creation; you are a co-creator with God. If Melchizedek is the High Priest and Jesus participated in that order. If Melchizedek is the person who must slay the lamb at the foundation of the world, then Melchizedek participated in releasing light and life. It was the Logos principle that allowed creation to come into existence.

In the mind of God, that Son later became Yeshua. Yeshua, the Son, opened up the realm for you to become a son. Melchizedek slew the Lamb, who was the Son so that the Lamb could become a human being and man could come into Sonship. The entire purpose of the sacrificial system is

117 John 1:1-3 in Greek
Ἐν ἀρχῇ ἦν ὁ λόγος καὶ ὁ λόγος ἦν πρὸς τὸν θεον καὶ θεὸς ἦν ὁ λόγος
En arche en ho Logos, kai ho logos en pros ton Theon kai Theos en ho Logos
118 https://en.wikipedia.org/wiki/Kenneth_E._Hagin

for you to participate and to come into Sonship as God the Father intended.

By participating in the release of creation into this realm, or by releasing divine intent into this realm, every child of God who is a son stands at the edge of divine consciousness and can look into the depths of God's being. Everything that God wants to do must first pass through the believer. As written in the Old Testament,

For the Lord GOD does nothing without revealing his secret to his servants the prophets.[119]

You, the believer and the son, are the one through whom God reveals His mind before doing anything in creation.

Let us move on to the fourth Melchizedek Principle, the Frequency of Kingship. The word *Melech*[120] means "kingship" in Hebrew. In simple gematria, its letters—Mem, Lamed, and Caph—add up to 90, which is the same as nine, a very significant number. Let me give you an interesting example of gematria. Look at the number 96. Can you see it? The 9 and the 6 are the same except one is facing up (9) and the other facing down (6). Nine represents the resurrected man, while 6 represents a man facing the earth. The difference between the two is three, which represents our triune God. Nine represents Adam, while 6 represents you.

So, *Melech*, the Principle of Kingship, refers to someone whose head reaches into heaven. That is what Israel means. Nine is associated with Israel—not the number itself, but the concept of Israel as the man whose head reaches into the sky, seeing God. The etymological meaning of the word *Israel* is

119 Amos 3:7
120 https://Biblehub.com/hebrew/4410.htm melukah מְלוּכָה : Kingship, Royalty https://Biblehub.com/hebrew/4428.htm melek מֶלֶךְ : King

Ish (man), *Resh* (head), and *El* (God). In other words, Israel means "the man who sees God" or "the head that sees God."

Likewise, the meaning of Melchizedek is *Melech Tzedek*.[121] As stated earlier, *Melech* is represented by the Hebrew letters Mem, Lamed, and Caph, which equal 40 + 30 + 20 or 90. Ninety is 9 using simple gematria. Tzedek is represented by the Hebrew letters Tsade, Dalet, and Caph, which equal 90 + 4 + 20 or 114. 114 adds up to 6 using simple gematria. The combination of the numbers 9 and 6 literally means the heavenly man who is manifested on earth. When you add 9 + 6, you get 15, which is the number of light.

If you replace 6, it becomes man as an earthly creature again. Every time you find the number 15 in Scripture, it is the number of light because 15 is the fundamental spectrum of light. Whenever light is mentioned in Scripture, the number 15 appears. Melchizedek is the frequency of a light being, and kingship is light. When a king dies, the first thing people say is that the light of that nation has gone out. They do not go to battle anymore, because the light of Israel is gone.[122]

The Frequency of Melchizedek represents the Principles of Sacrifice, Sonship, and Kingship. Sonship is based on DNA, while Kingship is a process of transmutation. This is because light has the capacity to change the nature of a thing. A true son and king has his head in heaven and his feet firmly planted on the earth. Many people in this movement have their heads in heaven. The problem is that their feet are not on the ground. Because of that, nothing can manifest because it becomes stuck in between the realms. A king is someone who has mastered the principle of developing his

---

121 https://Biblehub.com/hebrew/4442.htm Malki-tsedeq מַלְכִּי־צֶדֶק

122 2 Samuel 21:17

soul and expanding it, allowing the things he receives from God to flow into his physical body.

The problem with many believers is that they see Kingship as just a word, but it has to do with your soul. Without a prosperous soul, you cannot manifest your Kingship on earth. Kingship is not just a word. It is a state of being that actively requires the development of the soul. If your soul does not prosper, your finances will not prosper either. If you do not train your soul, your wealth, finances, and resources on earth will not prosper. This is because your soul blocks the manifestation of what you have seen from the other realm. If you do not focus on your soul, it will not grow. You may have spent a lot of time trying to develop your spirit, but it will not grow if your soul is not growing.

Concerning your spiritual development, your spirit is of God so there is nothing to grow there. You have spent so much time trying to grow something that was not meant to grow. You have forgotten what was meant to grow, what was meant to be opened. The Spirit of God travels on the frequency of the soul, which is exactly why God gave you a soul in the first place. But you have spent your entire Christian life cursing your soul. Society, the church, and you yourself have been wasting so much energy talking about just how terrible your soul is. You have taken all the wrongs of your old dead soul and transferred them to your new soul, which is a divine soul that has done nothing wrong. You have been cursing this brand new being, this baby from heaven. After spending 20 years of your Christian life cursing it, is it surprising that you are not manifesting anything? You are rendered spiritually impotent specifically because of the way you treated your soul. It is crying like a baby! Every time you confess your sins, you beat up your soul for something it never did. You have stifled the soul that came from heaven,

never allowing it to expand according to the pattern of the Spirit, which is God. Your real nature is sitting up there with all the things it brought from heaven, but you have stifled the code of your soul.

Nothing is wrong with your spirit! You were not born halfway; you are not an aborted fetus from heaven! You are real and your spirit is real. God actually lives in you, so the question remains, if God lives in you completely, why is your life messed up? Why can you not manifest anything? Why can you not create or invent anything? Why can you not change the world? The reason is you have messed up your soul. Unbelievers with dead souls spend a lot of time training their souls so that their bodies can function as gateways for the environment to manifest. But you have been spending your time beating up your soul. If you are a new being and your soul is new, why are you struggling? It is because your body was a participant in the scene of your old soul. Your soul is not the problem; it is your body. To deal with your body, God gave it the Holy Spirit. Your sin is embedded in your body and buried there. Again, your soul is not the problem because your soul is brand new. God is working to tune the frequency of your body so that it can function as the divine conduit for manifestation as it was always intended to be. Your spirit is God and your soul is saved. The only thing that needs to be redeemed is your body.[123]

The king's identity is not based on anything that is temporary or fleeting, but on a fundamental principle of being. The king's statements about himself are always a reflection of God's identity. God introduced Himself to Moses as "I am," and the same applies to a king. The king knows who he is, understanding his identity as an intrinsic foundation of his existence.

---

123 Romans 7:24; Romans 8:23

The Melchizedek Principle of Kingship is a process of intellection because it is a process of light. People generally associate intellection with intellectuality. However, intellection is the movement of the mind that allows it to bring new things out of everything it engages. Intellection is a movement; it is a flow.[124] The word intellectual[125] comes from the Latin word *intellectualis*. Intellectual does not refer to academics. Rather, it is a motion of the soul upon the mind, allowing the mind to open up to new possibilities whenever it touches something.

One of the reasons why the New Testament talks so much about the mind is because of where the king carries his crown, which is on his head. It is the light of the mind, which is the light of the soul. You should be among the most intellectual people in the world. This Melchizedek Principle is about opening up the head. You might think that your spiritual experience is not intellectual, but that is just not so. I am not saying that your spiritual experience is academic, but it *is* intellectual. Your experiences are an intellectual movement of your mind because it understands things it is not supposed to understand. *Intellection* is the mind invading blueprints, looking at, going through, and getting inside them to draw out new things. This is why, in Jewish mysticism, the Melchizedek Principle is one of scientific invention. Even the occultist knows that when they talk about the Melchizedek Principle, they are talking about the capacity to transmute, to change, to manifest, and to bring things here from another realm.

When we talk about kingship, our great example is King David. How many inventions did David have? There are 14

124 https://www.merriam-webster.com/dictionary/intellection
   https://www.etymonline.com/word/intellection
125 https://www.etymonline.com/search?q=intellectual

inventions written in your Bible that belong to King David.[126] How many inventions did Solomon have? Innumerable! We have people calling themselves kings who cannot invent anything, and who manifest nothing. If you call yourself a Melchizedek ministry, you are saying that your ministry is an incubation chamber for divine downloads and witty inventions.[127] You are saying your ministry is a place of Kingship, a place of Sonship, a place where we activate the Principle of Sacrifice. If it is not our own, it is the sacrifice of the Son of God that allows sons to be present and operate as sons and kings. In this way, our intellection process can allow the manifestation of new things so that the world becomes a better place. The whole idea is that if the mind of Christ is a principle of intellection, then the mind of a son has the capacity for expansiveness.

Let me tell you a little about Melchizedek. This being is able to take things and connect the future into the present. Remember, Melchizedek is man before man existed. God took this being from the moment in the future when we will be one and connected it to the point before creation making us act as one man. This released the blood and the light that allowed creation to come into existence. In other words, this is the body of Christ before Christ became a human being. In Hebrews, we read that Jesus said that a body had been prepared for Him. [128] He is referring to the Melchizedek body that Jesus picked up when He came into the world, the Melchizedek body that God prepared for Jesus. When we say, "I am a priest after the order of Melchizedek," we operate in that body. This is why I told you to give your loose change away. Melchizedek's sacrifice is always powerful. It taps into something from before creation. Start acting like a priest!

126 https://Biblearchaeologyreport.com/2021/06/11/top-ten-discoveries-related-to-david/

127 Proverbs 8:12

128 Hebrews 10:5

Stop acting like an ordinary human being! Everything you hold in your hand is cosmic. At all times, you ought to act like one who is changing the world.

This Melchizedek Principle allows for an interflow, an inflow and outflow, between man and God. Because we participated in the release of creation into creation, we are also an intrinsic part of the Melchizedek Principle. It is only through the Melchizedek Priesthood that the universe can be rectified. Jesus could not save the world if He did not join humanity and become a priest according to the order of Melchizedek because that is the only thing God ever made to rectify creation.

You can find this in the Levitical Priesthood. The Levitical Priesthood is only a shadow of the Melchizedek Priesthood. Many people try to get you into the Levitical Priesthood and bring you into the shadow instead of allowing you to operate in the real thing. Some of you are pretending to be Jews and want to fall under the Aaronic Priesthood, which is only a shadow, instead of embracing the real thing. You want to become Jews, but you cannot even be a good Gentile. This is a problem with many people in church. They want to be Jewish, but they cannot be. Jews themselves could not even keep the law, despite having it for thousands of years![129] Now you come around in your arrogance and say, "We are going to keep it all." You say, "I am keeping the feasts." How are the feasts being kept? Please explain to me.

Oh, you are building a sukkah inside your house with clothes. Is that a real sukkah? Who went up to the palm tree to cut the palm branches to bring it down for you to build an actual sukkah? Exactly what kind of sukkah are you building?[130] Remember, if you do not do it the right way,

129 Acts 15:10
130 https://tinyurl.com/35t7r96d

it is useless, and you are insulting the very One who gave the ordinances. You think that a sukkah is built only with tents and clothes? In my culture, we actually live in booths when we celebrate the Sukkot. We find a palm tree, cut down new palm leaves, and weave them together to make the roof. That is a true sukkah: a temporary dwelling that is no longer usable when the sun comes out. However, you can go ahead and celebrate the sukkah in your house with a tent. Just make sure to keep the inside clean and ensure that your feet do not touch the mud while doing the roof.

Did you know that the sukkah is one of the celebrations where the Israelites lived in the wilderness? It is not celebrated in the temple. Oh, sorry, did I just offend you? I had to explain this to all those people who want to be Jews, to all those people who are going to Israel to drive in their car where Jesus walked.

The Melchizedek Principle does not shy away from using nature and materiality as a way of expanding human consciousness. It allows nature to reveal the God that is hidden within. Every Melchizedek priest has access to pre-creation realities because this person, this priest, stands before the world was created. Melchizedek priests have access to the day *before* creation, enabling them to observe the mind of God in pre-creation reality.

The form is in the sacrifice and movement of the blood, which is the very light of the Lamb. Melchizedek has access to that, meaning he has simultaneous access to primordial wisdom and pre-creation reality. Do you remember when we discussed your soul? Your living soul is so powerful because it carries the records from before Adam was created *and* before he fell. Your living soul has no record of the fall, but your body does. There is no record of sin in your spirit because your spirit is God. Up until now, the way it has been working for you is that you have been trying to grow your spirit and rebuke your soul. You need to accept your spirit and grow your soul. Let the Holy Spirit work on your body as you willingly choose to subject your body to the Holy Spirit.

I am sure you are asking, what does he mean when speaking of pre-creation realities? The pre-creation reality is the man that was inside the mind of God before creation. This means that humanity was in God as a Son. It has always been God's intention to create a Son, to manifest a Son, to birth a Son into creation that will carry the fullness of God. This person begins to have the resonances, the sounds, the joyful exuberance of Divinity, and the intent of Divinity to create the world. This person knows the love of God, the perichoretic interaction of divine love, and the inter-penetrative principle of being. This person is able to enter into everything in nature and come out unscathed, drawing the divinity in it and manifesting it in the open because they are the bearers of the original scroll of Divine intentionality. Furthermore, because they have access to the innermost things happening inside of God, they themselves become the matrix. This is important because the matrix is the possible reconfiguration of nature at *any* level. In a sense, we can say that you are a divine crucible. When God wants to change the world, He does it inside of you. When He wants to change nature, He first does it inside of you. That is why God put all of nature in your physical body and works within you. Before nature changes, you always feel it. And if it is going to be healed, you get healed first because you are the microcosm of the macrocosm.

You are an embodiment of the whole universe. Now that you are a child of God, every cell of your body sings with the vibrational frequency of Divinity and the deliberate intentionality of the divine mind. When you think that is

how the world goes, your whole genetic system speaks of a world to come. The Melchizedek Principle is where prophecy meets Kingship—where prophecy *means* Kingship. Prophecy is no longer foretelling; it is a decree.

It is so. It is so. It is so.

Chapter 5

THE FREQUENCY
OF REST

I want you to know that everything I am discussing is within the following passage of Scripture.

Who being the brightness of His glory, and the express image of His person, and upholding all things by the word of His power, when He had by himself purged our sins, sat down on the right hand of the Majesty on high; Being made so much better than the angels, as He hath by inheritance obtained a more excellent name than they. For unto which of the angels said He at any time, Thou art my Son, this day have I begotten thee? And again, I will be to Him a Father, and He shall be to me a Son? And again, when He bringeth in the first begotten into the world, He saith, And let all the angels of God worship him. And of the angels He saith, Who maketh His angels spirits, and His ministers a flame of fire.[31]

By the way, angels were not originally created as spirits. They become spirits through obedience. That is why demons are not considered spirits. I want to make this crystal clear so that you will not get stuck on this point if you have been following this false doctrine. Consider this: demons have no positive energy. As in most cultures, the word "spirit" represents a vitalizing principle. This is because the Hebrew language is an animistic language[132] and it does not differentiate between demons and spirits. Anything that exists is considered a spirit, whether it is good or bad. This is one reason I believe God allowed the New Testament to be written in Greek. Greek is the only language that has specific words to distinguish between a demon and a spirit.

The Greek language offers a clearer understanding of what the Hebrew language may struggle to explain. Many make assumptions about the difference between Greek and Hebrew thinking, but these assumptions are often based on limited exposure or a lack of understanding of Greek culture. Greek culture, including its reasoning and argumentation, is circular in nature, not linear. People often make blanket statements about Greek thinking without truly understanding it. As a result, they are perceived as uninformed. It is essential to ask questions, read primary sources such as Homer,[133] and familiarize oneself with Greek mythology and culture to understand it more deeply.

The Greek language, with its capacity to communicate complex ideas and abstract concepts, was chosen by God to be the language in which the bulk of the New Testament was written. The Greek language has the capacity to articulate

132 Animism (from Latin: anima meaning ‹breath, spirit, life›) is the belief that objects, places, and creatures all possess a distinct spiritual essence. Animism perceives all things—animals, plants, rocks, rivers, weather systems, human handiwork, and in some cases words, as animated and alive. (Source Wikipedia)

133 https://en.wikipedia.org/wiki/Homer

what the Hebrew language was unable to express. Although Hebrew is also an animistic language, it struggles with making distinctions between different types of spirits and entities, simply labeling them as good or bad. Both Hebrew and Greek languages have their limitations and strengths, and neither was intended to have a purely logical understanding of God.

The Rabbis considered the Greek language to be closer to their thoughts than any other Gentile language. I like hearing people say things that are not true because they believe that being inspired by God means they have knowledge. Unfortunately, this kind of thinking is far too prevalent. People think that because they have inspiration from God, they know everything. However, this is a misunderstanding of this verse in 1 John:

...You have no need that anyone should teach you.[134]

This should not be understood as knowing everything, but rather knowing God. You do not need anyone to teach you anything about God, but you do need someone to teach you about the things of the field, such as how certain leaves can be harmful to you. If you do not learn about these things and start eating random herbs in the bush, you will have a truly bad day. Bear in mind, I am not being rationalistic; I am actually being very biblical. It is amazing that God sends human beings to other human beings to explain something to them, even though they have just encountered God. Do you remember what happened to Paul on the road?

You have to balance the Scripture. You cannot take one thread of Scripture and say that it is all you need. Scripture is like a sweater. Scripture is an intertwining thread. If you remove one, you do not have a sweater; you just have a rope.

---

134 1 John 2:27

The reason we call certain entities *demons* is they were not confirmed in their obedience. Do you remember this verse?

Who makes His angels spirits, His ministers a flame of fire.[135]

It does not say God created or formed them as spirits; it says that He *makes* them spirits. The angels who did not obey were not confirmed in the nature of God. They were not made a spirit, but instead were released into the realm of existence. They lack the ability to give life. As a result, they do not possess vitalizing principles. Demons live as vampires, relying on the energy and strength they receive from human beings. They are, in essence, leeches.

I stopped engaging with demons a long time ago when I realized what they were doing. They were using my attention, focus, and energy to bolster their own power. When I understood this, I simply turned my attention away from them and focused on Jesus Christ instead. As a result, demons have not approached me. It is amazing to see people come to church and say that they are fighting demons when everyone else is worshiping God. If you are worshiping Jesus and the Father, why would demons want to be in your presence? Demons are not in anyone else's presence while they are genuinely worshiping God. You must have brought them with you. Demons cannot reside in a place where Jesus is present. No demon can stand before Jesus Christ without trembling.[136] If you are focusing on worshiping Christ, there should be no place for demons.

I learned this lesson a long time ago. For example, at the church in Venice, we do not allow demons to be present. This is not because we do not believe in their existence,

135 Psalm 104:4
136 James 2:19

but because we have established boundaries to protect the church. I have sympathy for any demon that tries to enter, in a good way.

Now, let us continue reading from the book of Hebrews.

> And again, when He bringeth in the first begotten into the world, He saith, And let all the angels of God worship him. And of the angels He saith, Who maketh His angels spirits, and His ministers a flame of fire. But unto the Son He saith, Thy throne, oh God, is for ever and ever: a sceptre of righteousness is the sceptre of thy kingdom. Thou hast loved righteousness, and hated iniquity; therefore God, even thy God, hath anointed thee with the oil of gladness above thy fellows. And, Thou, Lord, in the beginning hast laid the foundation of the earth; and the heavens are the works of thine hands: They shall perish; but thou remainest; and they all shall wax old as doth a garment; And as a vesture shalt thou fold them up, and they shall be changed: but thou art the same, and thy years shall not fail. But to which of the angels said He at any time, Sit on my right hand, until I make thine enemies thy footstool? Are they not all ministering spirits, sent forth to minister for them who shall be heirs of salvation?[137]

Let us skip ahead to Hebrews 2.

> For unto the angels hath He not put in subjection the world to come, whereof we speak. But one in a certain place testified, saying, What is man, that thou art mindful of him? Or the Son of Enosh, that thou visitest him? Thou madest Him a little lower than Elohim; thou crownedst Him with glory and honour, and didst set Him over the works of thy hands: Thou hast put all things in subjection under His feet. For in that He put all in subjection under

137 Hebrews 1:6-14 (KJV)

him, He left nothing that is not put under him. But now we see not yet all things put under him. But we see Jesus, who was made a little lower than the Elohim for the suffering of death, crowned with glory and honour; that He by the grace of God may taste death for every human being. For it became him, for whom are all things, and by whom are all things, in bringing many sons unto glory, to make the captain of their salvation perfect through sufferings. For both He that sanctifieth and they who are sanctified are all of one. For which cause He is not ashamed to call them brethren.[138]

This is the whole crux of the Melchizedek Principle. The one who sanctifies, and the one who is being sanctified, are one.

Saying, I will declare thy name unto my brethren, in the midst of the congregation will I sing praise unto thee. And again, I will put my trust in him. And again, Behold I and the children which the Lord God hath given me. Forasmuch then as the children are partakers of flesh and blood, He also himself likewise took part of the same; that through death He might destroy Him that had the power of death, that is, the devil. And deliver them who through fear of death were all their lifetime subject to bondage.[139]

Therefore, we see that the victory over death is not in the spirit but in the human body. The key to defeating death lies within the human body! The true challenge that humanity faces is the fear of death. This fear is the reason many people do not leave their physical bodies or ascend into heaven. It is not just an ordinary fear, but the fear of death that holds people back from experiencing life to its fullest.

---

138 Hebrews 2:5-11 (KJV)
139 Hebrews 2:12-15 (KJV)

> For verily He took not on Him the nature of angels; but He took on Him the seed of Abraham. Wherefore in all things it behoved Him to be made like unto His brethren, that He might be a merciful and faithful High Priest in things pertaining to God, to make reconciliation for the sins of the people.[140]

There are no angelic beings included in salvation. That is the first error of most Universalists. Salvation is not offered to angels. Jesus came in the flesh; He did not take on the nature of angels. The beings that God came to save in the world are humans, not angels. It is a false notion. I will say again that Origen[141] actually believed that the Satan is going to be saved. Origen was from Sudan in Egypt, not Europe. He was from Upper Egypt, an African! You will not find any African who says that the Satan is going to be saved. It is not even in our vocabulary. Origen was exploring the possibility of salvation in that context.

> Wherefore in all things it behoved Him to be made like unto His brethren, that He might be a merciful and faithful High Priest in things pertaining to God, to make reconciliation for the sins of the people. For in that He himself hath suffered being tempted, He is able to succour them that are tempted. Wherefore, Holy brethren, partakers of the heavenly calling, consider the Apostle and High Priest of our profession, Christ Jesus; Who was faithful to Him that appointed him, as also Moses was faithful in all His house. For this man was counted worthy

---

140 Hebrews 2:16-17 (KJV)

141 https://en.wikipedia.org/wiki/Origen
https://www.christianitytoday.com/history/people/scholarsandscientists/origen.html

of more glory than Moses, inasmuch as He who hath builded the house hath more honour than the house.

For every house is builded by some man; but He that built all things is God. And Moses verily was faithful in all His house, as a servant, for a testimony of those things which were to be spoken after; But Christ as a Son over His own house; whose house are we, if we hold fast the confidence and the rejoicing of the hope firm unto the end.[142]

It is funny how people ignore simple adverbial, adjectival, and conditional phrases in the Bible. The word "if" is part of the text when God says to Israel "If" you obey and "If" you keep the covenant. God made these statements, not men. You cannot remove something from the mouth of God and put your own words in there. "If" is a crucial part of these statements.

If we hold fast the confidence and the rejoicing of the hope firm unto the end. Wherefore as the Holy Ghost saith, To day if ye will hear His voice, Harden not your hearts, as in the provocation, in the day of temptation in the wilderness: When your fathers tempted me, proved me, and saw my works forty years. Wherefore I was grieved with that generation, and said, They do always err in their heart; and they have not known my ways. So I sware in my wrath, They shall not enter into my rest. So I swore that they will not enter my rest. They shall not take heed there for bread and let there be in any of you an evil heart of unbelief.[143]

Did you read the text above? If so, what is the problem? How are you saved? You can argue like the Calvinists that the

---

142 Hebrews 2:17-3:6 (KJV)
143 Hebrews 3:6-12 (KJV)

only way you can say "yes" to God is if God makes you. But if God makes you say, "Yes," you have not actually said, "Yes." It is like the child whom the mother tells to sit, "Johnny, sit! Johnny, sit! Johnny, sit!" But despite the mother's commands, the child is still standing. The mother then picks him up and places him in a chair while she says, "Now you are sitting," but the child replies, "No, outside I am sitting, but inside I am standing." Your "yes" must come from your own heart and through your own faith.

Take heed, brethren, lest there be in any of you an evil heart of unbelief, in departing from the living God. But exhort one another daily, while it is called To day; lest any of you be hardened through the deceitfulness of sin. For we are made partakers of Christ, if we hold the beginning of our confidence steadfast unto the end;[144]

We need to learn how to read Scripture in a way that allows us to see all of it. One of the challenges we face with Scripture is that we tend to pick and choose verses rather than reading the whole text. Just because you really like select verses does not make you a theologian. It is only by understanding the entire text and putting the pieces together that you can truly become a theologian. What makes theologians different from a lay reader is that they do not cherry-pick verses. They recognize that the individual verses themselves are not inspired by God.

The Hebrew Bible was not divided into chapters and verses. The division into verses was not something inspired by God. I recall when I first started reading the Bible in Hebrew; I would go to the synagogue and be asked to read. In order to fulfill that responsibility, I would have to spend the night before finding the text of the book of Isaiah so that I could read it the next day. This is because there were

144 Hebrews 3:12-14 (KJV)

no verses in the text. To this day, I still do not know how to memorize the Bible in verses. However, I know the Scripture very well. If I tell you something that is not in the Bible, you can be sure that it is not there. This is because I have read it over 40 times, not only in English but also in Hebrew and Greek.

If you come to argue with me about the meaning of Scripture, make sure you have your facts straight. If you are not reading the Bible in Hebrew and Greek, any argument you make with me will be nonsense. I will ask you what the original text says and how it is structured. Christians are the only ones who do not read their own holy book in its original language. They often think they know more than the original text. I am sorry to say this, but I have told my church that everyone needs to learn Hebrew. If we want to argue, let us do so based on the text, not just on our opinions of it.

I really have a problem with Christians in this area. Why is it that Muslims can read Arabic and Hindus can read Sanskrit, but Christians who consider themselves knowledgeable about the faith know nothing of the original language? When you look at the interpretations of the Bible, most of what is referred to as translations are actually interpretations. I must say that, in this regard, I respect the Muslims. They believe that every translation is an interpretation. If we are going to have an argument, let us have it based on the original text. I say this because I want to make a point, so please do not take offense.

But exhort one another daily, while it is called To day; lest any of you be hardened through the deceitfulness of sin. For we are made partakers of Christ, if we hold the beginning of our confidence stedfast unto the end. While it is said, To-day if ye will hear His voice, harden not your hearts, as in the provocation. For some, when they had

heard, did provoke: howbeit not all that came out of Egypt by Moses. But with whom was He grieved forty years? Was it not with them that had sinned, whose carcasses fell in the wilderness?[145]

You need to understand that the natural world is a reflection of the upper realm. It is just like your physical body, which is a reflection of a supernal principle. Your pineal gland[146] is known as the alchemical stone. It is the transmutational principle in your body, the smallest thing in your brain, and the only one.

The stone is called the Even HaShatiya and is a foundationstone[147] of your being. It is what Jacob slept on in the desert when he saw the ladder to heaven. It is the stone in the temple where the Ark of the Covenant sat. However, it is not a simple rock; it is actually a liquid. It is the foundational plasma of the universe. This is why you have a pineal gland. It is the substance connecting you to the foundation stone of the universe.[148]

Jacob placed his head on a stone, or rather, his pineal gland. That was how he could alter his consciousness. The substance produced by the pineal gland alters consciousness and allows the individual to move up and down through the realms without the need for drugs.

---

145 Hebrews 3:12-17 (KJV)

146 https://en.wikipedia.org/wiki/Pineal_gland
https://www.cityofluz.com/dmt-kabbalah-pineal-gland/
https://tinyurl.com/55ajabbp

147 https://tinyurl.com/4spx3569 In the Temple, the ark rested directly on the "Even Hashetiyah"—the Shetiya stone, which is the foundation point of the entire world. In the second Temple there was no ark, only the Shetiya stone.

148 Furthermore, according to the Talmud, the world itself was created from the Even Hashetiya - the foundation stone over which the Holy of Holies of the Temple was built. https://tinyurl.com/2xw9p7bt

And to whom sware He that they should not enter into His rest, but to them that believed not? So we see that they could not enter in because of unbelief.[149]

One aspect of the Melchizedek Frequency is known as the Frequency of Faith. I understand that you might have a preconceived notion about what faith is, but I would like to present a different perspective on it.

Let us therefore fear, lest, a promise being left us of entering into His rest, any of you should seem to come short of it.[150]

One of the biggest problems we face is the lack of rest. We may claim to walk in peace; but in reality, we do not have any inner peace. One time when I was teaching about inner peace, someone said I was teaching Hinduism. I responded by saying, "Please, do not have inner peace so you will not be considered a Hindu." It seems that we have a tendency to worry, be anxious, and be agitated so we can be good Christians. We tend to criticize concepts and ideas that violate our religious understanding without checking it against Scripture. We try to find reasons why something will not work so that it fits with our current understanding. However, this is often not based on Scripture. In this example, the Bible says that the peace we are given is beyond comprehension and surpasses understanding.[151] In my book *Opening the Gates of Glory*,[152] the chapter on the beatitudes discusses the concept of internal peace for Christians. The universe was created from a still point of divinity where nothing moves, similar to what happens in the throne room.

---

149 Hebrews 3:18-19 (KJV)

150 Hebrews 4:1 (KJV)

151 Philippians 4:7

152 Dr. Adonijah Ogbonnaya, *Opening the Gates of Glory: The Beatific Life* (Venice, CA: Seraph Creative, 2020)

The sea appears like glass because it is unaffected by the change of time.

> For unto us was the gospel preached, as well as unto them: but the word preached did not profit them, not being mixed with faith in them that heard it.

> For we which have believed do enter into rest, as he said, As I have sworn in my wrath, if they shall enter into my rest: although the works were finished from the foundation of the world. For he spake in a certain place of the seventh day on this wise, And God did rest the seventh day from all his works. And in this place again, If they shall enter into my rest. Seeing therefore it remaineth that some must enter therein, and they to whom it was first preached entered not in because of unbelief:

> Again, he limiteth a certain day, saying in David, To day, after so long a time; as it is said, Today if ye will hear his voice, harden not your hearts. For if Jesus[153] had given them rest, then would he not afterward have spoken of another day.[154]

You are a believer because you have activated the Melchizedek Principle of Faith, a principle that overrides unbelief, and rewrites and rewires your tendency towards doubt about the things of God. My Jewish background involves simply reading the Scripture, which often speaks for itself and does not require a secondary interpretation.

---

153 Although the KJV uses the name "Jesus" in the verse, many other versions use the name "Joshua." The word in the original Greek is Ἰησοῦς (Iēsous). Using the name "Joshua" is based on an interpretation of the text, not a literal translation. You can see that using the name "Joshua" confuses the meaning of the text. However, the context makes much more sense using the name "Jesus." Jesus has said that He will give us rest, but according to this passage, He has not yet let us into that rest. Since it did not come with Christ, that day is still coming.

154 Hebrews 4:2-8 (KJV)

For example, when the Scripture says, "do not lie," it means just that: do not lie.

Contrary to popular belief, the land of Israel is not a land of rest. Despite any theology or shouting to the contrary, Israel is a land of war and the conflict has never ended. It is not the land that is the problem, but the people.

There remaineth therefore a rest to the people of God. For he that is entered into his rest, he also hath ceased from his own works, as God did from his.[155]

Scripture really commands only one true work—to labor and to come to a place of rest. This is the greatest work you can do because this is where the enemy attacks you. According to the Melchizedek Principle, rest is the place where true creativity emerges and where higher, even ultimate, consciousness can be achieved. This state of rest is where divine technologies flow into the realm of creation. You struggle with manifesting your creativity, despite having great ideas, because you have not found that place of rest. This means that the Sabbath is not the last day of creation, but rather the first day. It is the beginning. It is the day *before* creation.

Think about this for a moment. God rested. So, if God was not at rest before He started creating, He could not have been at rest after creation. The rest was ahead, but also before the first day of creation. I have teachings[156] that discuss the interior nature of God and the stillness of the divine within the context of divinity; I suggest you look them up. Joy arises from stillness, and then comes ecstasy, followed by creation.

155 Hebrews 4:9-10 (KJV)
156   See www.aactev8.com for more information about teachings.

~ 136 ~

Creation emerges from a place of stillness and silence, the very silence and stillness that is in the depth of God.

One thing we often forget is just how important rest is for creativity. I am not talking about lazy rest. I am talking about a deliberate restful posture that creates an empty space for something new to fill. The purpose of driving your mind towards nothingness is not so that you end up with nothing. It is to create an empty space from which something new can emerge.

I am sure that right about now, you are wondering just what prevents the Melchizedek Principle from working? The answer is simple: unbelief. That is why I keep returning to the will and the capacity of man in my teachings. If you remove faith and belief, you remove the capacity of man to create.

Let us labor to enter into the rest, lest any man fall after the example of unbelief. For the word of God is quick, and powerful, and sharper than any twoedged sword, piercing even to the dividing asunder of soul and spirit, and of the joints and marrow, and is a discerner of the thoughts and intents of the heart. Neither is there any creature that is not manifest in His sight: but all things are naked and opened unto the eyes of Him with whom we have to do. Seeing then that we have a great High Priest, that is passed into the heavens, Jesus the Son of God, let us hold fast our profession.[157]

Before Jesus came into the world, it was God's intention that everyone connected with Melchizedek would not just minister on earth, but in the heavenly realm. That means the

---

157 Hebrews 4:11-14 (KJV)

sons of God are connected with the projection of Divinity and the living garment we know as the being of Melchizedek.

Seeing then that we have a great High Priest, that is passed into the heavens, Jesus the Son of God, let us hold fast our profession. For we have not an High Priest which cannot be touched with the feeling of our infirmities; but was in all points tempted like as we are, yet without sin. Let us therefore come boldly unto the throne of grace, that we may obtain mercy, and find grace to help in time of need.

For every High Priest taken from among men is ordained for men in things pertaining to God, that He may offer both gifts and sacrifices for sins: Who can have compassion on the ignorant, and on them that are out of the way; for that He himself also is compassed with infirmity. And by reason hereof He ought, as for the people, so also for himself, to offer for sins. And no man taketh this honour unto himself, but He that is called of God, as was Aaron.

So also Christ glorified not himself to be made an High Priest; but He that said unto him, Thou art my Son, to day have I begotten thee. As He saith also in another place, Thou art a priest for ever after the order of Melchizedek.[158]

Here you see that Jesus is not Melchizedek, because Jesus became a member of Melchizedek's order. He was actually initiated into the order of Melchizedek. Again, the Lord Jesus Christ is *not* Melchizedek. You can argue until tomorrow, but Jesus is still not Melchizedek, and Melchizedek is not Jesus.

---

158 Hebrews 4:14-5:6 (KJV)

Jesus is a member of the order of Melchizedek, and we are the ones who initiated Jesus.

It is amazing that God subjected Himself to us, so that we could initiate Jesus. What did you think would happen to God when He became a human being? Humans needed to teach Him what it means to be human, in both good and bad ways. It is man who taught God how to be man; therefore, it is man who initiates the Son of God into the priesthood. The Melchizedek Priesthood is a human priesthood; it is humanity serving as God's own priests.

Who in the days of His flesh, when He had offered up prayers and supplications with strong crying and tears unto Him that was able to save Him from death, and was heard in that He feared; Though He were a Son, yet learned He obedience by the things which He suffered....[159]

I will delve more deeply into the Frequency of Suffering in another volume. However, I wanted to point out briefly here that many of us waste the power of our sufferings and tears by complaining. Every time you complain, you lose the energetic system of your own suffering. Your suffering is transmutative; it literally gives you the power to change things. This is Christianity 101, right? Jesus suffered to transmute you and me. Therefore, a Christian does not suffer in vain, unless they are blind to the power of their own suffering. Do not waste your tears; do not waste your suffering.

And being made perfect, He became the author of eternal salvation unto all them that obey him; Called of God an High Priest after the order of Melchizedek. Of

---

159 Hebrews 5:7-8 (KJV)

whom we have many things to say, and hard to be uttered, seeing ye are dull of hearing.

For when for the time ye ought to be teachers, ye have need that one teach you again which be the first principles of the oracles of God; and are become such as have need of milk, and not of strong meat. For every one that useth milk is unskilful in the word of righteousness: for He is a babe. But strong meat belongeth to them that are of full age, even those who by reason of use have their senses exercised to discern both good and evil.

Therefore leaving the principles of the doctrine of Christ, let us go on unto perfection; not laying again the foundation of repentance from dead works, and of faith toward God, Of the doctrine of baptisms, and of resurrection of the dead, and of eternal judgment.[160]

Why is the resurrection of the dead referred to as something elementary? It is considered a first principle, but why is it called foundational or elementary? It is because the resurrection is meant to put an end to death. At this point in Christianity, we should no longer be talking about dying or the resurrection of the dead.

Death has been removed from the earth *twice*. Yes, I did just write that. Death has been removed twice from the earth. The first time was when death reigned from Adam to Moses. On the day of Pentecost when Israel was supposed to accept God, God removed death from creation. However, Israel allowed it to return. The Bible says that death reigned from Adam to Moses[161] even over those who did not sin according to the sin of Adam, including children whose sins had not been activated. Death even reigned over those who lived a

160 Hebrews 5:9-6:2 (KJV)
161 Romans 5:14

righteous life and whose sins had not been activated. Moses was the last man over whom death should have been able to reign because immortality was activated during his life. Moses brought that immortality to the Jews on the day of Pentecost, but they rejected it.

You know that Moses did not die, right? Did the Lord say it or did the writer say it? Read the text again in Deuteronomy 34 again.[162] It was God who spoke to Aaron and said, "Bring Aaron up so that he might be stripped of his garment and die."[163] Aaron's garment was made according to the pattern that Moses saw in the heavens. The question is who was wearing that garment and what did Moses see? This question is important because we need to understand what type of priest Moses was. We know Moses was a High Priest because he initiated Aaron. You cannot initiate someone unless you are a High Priest yourself. So, the next question is what type of priest was Moses? Moses was also a king. It says so in the Bible:

And he was a king in Jeshurun.[164]

Moses was the only one who was both a king and a priest in Israel. No one on earth made Moses a priest and a king. Therefore, Moses was not an Aaronic priest; he was a priest after the order of Melchizedek.

I like the Bible. Sometimes when I teach people, I ask them, "Where is it in the Bible?" And then, I engage in a conversation about it. I love Scripture. If you spend any amount of time around me, one thing you will learn is that I am Biblically based and Christ-centric. I take the Lord Jesus Christ seriously because if I do not, I should leave

162 Deuteronomy 34:5-7
163 Numbers 20:26-28
164 Deuteronomy 34:7

Christianity and return to Judaism. It is amazing to me, and not in a good way, that some people in this movement even suggest that there are other ways to God and that the Messiah is not the only way. They try to justify things by making it seem as if Christ is just a suggestion from God. Be careful though because the Lord Jesus Christ said,

> "I am the way, and the truth, and the life. No one comes to the Father except through me."[165]

He also said,

> "I told you that you would die in your sins, for unless you believe that I am he you will die in your sins."[166]

I do not play with the Lord Jesus Christ. I may not have all the answers, but those two things are not up for personal interpretation.

When we talk about Scripture, there is a canon. I do not accept your Western canon, but I do agree that your canon is Scripture. Do you understand the difference? What I am saying is that I accept your 66 books as being canonical, but I believe it is too small. My canon is bigger, which allows me greater latitude to experience the spiritual realm than your canon does. I am an Ethiopian Christian, an African Christian, and we have our own canon. We do not follow the Protestant canon. I encourage all Africans to return to the Ethiopian canon so that we can read the Book of Enoch, the Book of Jubilees, the Book of Jasher, and the Gospel of Peter. The purpose for having a canon is so that you and I have a basis for our arguments. We do not argue based only on our experiences because if we do, we will end up in conflict with each other. However, if we have a common set of texts to

165 John 14:6
166 John 8:24

reference, we can at least begin with a common vocabulary. For example, we can both come to agreement that "die" means "die."

We must begin our argument from a basis of linguistic agreement. The conventional language is the language of discussion and if you are to create a new word, you must define it in a way that is understandable to those with whom you are conversing. God did not offer a suggestion when He said, "The day you eat this, you will surely die." When God says, "die," you die. To be raised from the dead is to be resurrected with a new body.

This is part of the Melchizedek Principle. All Melchizedek-oriented priests and prophets in Scripture were allowed to make sacrifices only if they were also priests. Only Levites were allowed to make sacrifices in Israel. So, if you see Elijah making a sacrifice, it means that he was both a priest and a prophet.[167] The question you need to ask is who made Elijah a priest when he was not a Levite? Clearly, Elijah was working from a different lineage. This same idea can be applied to David.[168]

Melchizedek priests can be found throughout Scripture,[169] and almost all of them did not die. They were transmuted or raised. There is a saying among Jews that may not be familiar to you. During certain ceremonies, we say, "David the king is not dead."[170] No one can explain why Israel gathers for secret meetings and makes this statement. However, the Bible states

167 1 Kings 18:33

168 2 Samuel 6:17

169 Adam, Seth, Noah, Enoch, Melchizedek, Abraham, Joseph, Moses, Job, Elijah, David, The High Priest Joshua, John the Baptist, Jesus

170 A prayer from The voice of the Turtledove called «Od Yosef Chai».
http://israel613.com/books/KOL_HATOR.pdf
Od Yesef Chai page 88
https://tinyurl.com/yckyxpvd

that David died. So why does Israel shout that David is not dead? It is because David is an embodiment of the Messiah and a priest after the order of Melchizedek.[171] David's spirit is alive; he even talks about ascending to heaven in the Bible.

In David's last prayer, he was raised up on high. Some translators have referred to him as the man who was enthroned, but this is not what the original Hebrew says. The Bible states that David was raised up to heaven,[172] indicating that he practiced ascension. King David even wrote psalms for ascending.[173] Therefore, his priesthood did not originate on earth. The priesthood that David organized in the temple came from another dimension and it was deliberately organized in such a way that every gateway of the earth's orientation towards other dimensions was controlled by David and his angels. The temple was built for the specific purposes of controlling dimensions, and enabling both inter- and intra-dimensional travel.[174]

The temple was not built just for making sacrifices. The blood in the temple was used as a way of transporting and traveling between dimensions. The light in the life of the animal was the way of going from this place to another. If we truly knew our identity, our way of operating would be quite different.

Elijah, a priest after the order of Melchizedek, went to heaven with a redeemed body that was transmuted into the Melchizedek body. This makes it a false theology to say that he will come back to die. The evangelical theology that holds this belief is a lie. Why would God bring someone who is

---

171 Psalm 110:4; Hebrews 5:6

172 2 Samuel 23:1

173 There are 15 Psalms that are called the songs of ascent. These are Psalms 120-134

174 This is the reason all ley lines on earth are running to Jerusalem

already in heaven, dancing with angels, back to earth to die especially when he has already overcome corruption by going through the flames of the chariots of God? Elijah's body was changed into the principle of light and fire. The idea that the two witnesses have to be Elijah and Enoch is highly questionable.

Enoch's world was already judged, and Enoch was a priest after the order of Melchizedek just like Abraham. There were no Levitical priests in the world at that time. The only real priest was the one Abraham met. Abraham was sowing into all of humanity, participating in the priesthood of humanity. Therefore, he was allowed to shadow that priesthood upon the face of the earth.

It is amazing what our Father has done. I have read the book of Hebrews repeatedly because I know it was written by a Jewish mystic. There is so much Jewish mysticism in the book of Hebrews that it is not even funny. I said that death has been removed from the earth twice and that those who know and understand the technology can access it. It was removed when Moses died. So, if Moses died, why was an angel fighting over his body? Can you imagine God fighting over a dead thing? We are talking about the same God who told the priest not to touch a dead body. Moses' body was in suspended animation and could not die, no matter what happened. Moses' body could not die because God had taken Moses while he was still alive, altering his genetic structure with the imprint of God's hand. Your hand contains the code of your being. In fact, every part of your body is embedded in your palm. Your palm is a complete representation of your body.[175] Why do you think pagans are so interested in palm reading? They read your hand to know your fate. But God says they should not because they are giving over access to

175   Isaiah 49:16

their inner self. In Chinese medicine, they know exactly what parts of your hands to use to affect your organs; they can actually heal your inner organs from the palm of your hand.

The Bible says,

**For he will command his angels concerning you
to guard you in all your ways.**

**On their hands they will bear you up,
lest you strike your foot against a stone.**[176]

They will use the record embedded in your hands to guide you. That is why you raise your hands when you worship. When Moses asked God to show him His glory,[177] God said no because, if He had shown him, Moses would disappear into Him. God wants a reflexive process between Him and us; He wants to know Himself as us, not just as Himself. God told Moses there was a rock near Him, and He would pass by Moses and transfer the life of God into Moses' body with the palm of His hand. That rock is the Lord Jesus Christ. By pressing Moses into the person of Christ, Moses actually experienced the resurrection.

The divine nature has been transferred twice since man was created. The first time was when God transferred the palm of His hand into the life of Moses. That was the first time God touched man since Adam. And when He comes, He will have experienced the resurrection due to the resurrection power. God put Moses in the garden tomb before Jesus even got there, and then He brought Moses out so that his body was completely transmuted. Moses could not die. That is why, at 120 years old, Moses' eyes did not go dim, his bones did not break, his skin did not change, and he had the same

176 Psalm 91:12
177 Exodus 33:18

bodily strength.[178] There were several people in the Bible who experienced the same thing. At the age of 80, Caleb said, "My body is still as strong as it was when I was 20."[179]

Moses comes out of that tradition. If Moses' whole body was translucent, what kind of body do you think Moses had? Moses walked around Israel with a light body. He had become a Cherubim; his whole being changed. Moses' body had the capacity for self-renewal. Because of this translucence in his body, God did not want him to enter the Promised Land. It was not just because he struck the rock. God did not want him to enter into the Promised Land with a transmuted, redeemed, transformed, and translucent Melchizedek body. If he had, the people would have worshiped Moses as God, making him a danger to Israel. Moses would have looked like a watcher.

God told Moses that He did not want him to be tempted. He had already started talking crazy because Moses did not glorify God, not because he struck the rock." Essentially, God said, "You have already started talking silly! You are talking crazy, so you need to come home." So Moses' body was suspended. It was on earth, but it was not buried. The Bible specifically says, "And God buried him."[180] Think about this. When does God touch a dead body and bury it in the grave? Furthermore, to this day, no one knows where God buried Moses because he was not on earth. He was in a separate space, suspended.

When the Lord Jesus Christ came, the secret of God was beginning to be revealed. The satanic system, fallen angels, became aware that God had created a human body that could not die. They realized that this creation was the divine

178 Deuteronomy 34:5-7
179 Joshua 14:11
180 Deuteronomy 34:6

embodiment of God. And they knew that if they could find a body that would not die, they could draw from its divine and eternal vitality. God realized that the secret was coming out. So He commanded Michael to retrieve the body of Moses. Remember, an angel would not carry a dead body. Michael went to retrieve Moses' body specifically because it was still alive, held in suspended animation.

At that moment, Moses was just a soul without a body in heaven. If his body had not been restored to him, Moses would not have been able to visit the Messiah with Elijah. God restored Moses' soul to his body and took him back to heaven. The meeting between Jesus and Moses on the mount was only possible because Moses' body had been infused with life. The same thing happened to Elijah, who also participated in the resurrection before the actual event. They did not have to die to experience a resurrected life.

Death was defeated with Moses because he was the first person to walk on earth with a real, light-infused, body. All other people who were taken by God were transformed and whisked away. Moses came out of God with a unique light-infused body and proceeded to walk with Israel for over 20 years. Moses literally walked on earth with this body.

CHAPTER 5: The Frequency of Rest

Chapter 6

THE FREQUENCY
OF RESPECT

I love the Scriptures, and I love the Lord Jesus Christ. I love the Lord Jesus Christ because the Scriptures are the written effluence of His nature. The Scriptures are not just letters. If you read them merely as letters, you will lose a lot. Scripture is the written effulgence of His being, the effluxes of His being. It is the mystery of God captured in black and white. When we talk about the Scripture in Judaism, we say it is black fire on white fire; or white fire on black fire, depending on who you ask.

The reason I read the whole Scripture is that I am not just picking out one thing. As I wrote earlier, one of the greatest problems in Christian theology and the Christian church as a whole is that we pick out particular verses and do not look at the text in context. I can go into the Scriptures and prove many things, just like I did earlier with the bridal paradigm. We cannot continue picking out certain texts and placing them out of context while simultaneously ignoring all the other Scriptures that actually speak of sons. The church needs to break away from the broken doctrine that says being the wife of Christ is the highest principle in Christianity. I know I have repeated myself a few times, but let that show you just how serious, and how utterly destructive and dangerous this problem is.

We need to take the text in its full context. Professors of homiletics and hermeneutics used to say, "Texts without context are pretext." Many people in the church have developed the bad habit of quoting verses without citing the whole word. You should quote the Scripture in its full context, keeping in mind the culture in which it is located. In this way, when you are challenged, you will not just pick out a single verse from within the text.

Let me give you an example. A man walked from Los Angeles to Nashville, and when he arrived, he talked to his wife. Verse one: "A man walked to Nashville." Verse three: "He talked to his wife." We do this same thing with our Holy Scripture. We take one of those verses and make it an idea, and then we ignore the rest. That is not theology. That is not biblical study.

We talk about many things that are not in the Bible. Ninety percent of the ordinary and common theology known in the church does not grow from the Bible, but from opinions. This is because most people have not taken the time to study

the whole text before they speak; they just study a single topic. Studying one topic is not the same as studying the whole Scripture. That is why in seminary school, they always tell you to focus on the exegetical message in depth, not just topical messages. The point is to take a text from Scripture, read it, draw from within the text, and do not impose on the text. In other words, do not try to force your own religious perspectives on the text.

I was a professor of homiletics and taught theology for many years. When I observe how people handle Scriptures, I wonder why they have no respect. Why do they think they can pick out a single verse of Scripture and make it into a theology, all the while ignoring the other 10,000 verses? This is a serious form of disrespect. If someone took a single aspect of your life and used it to judge you, you would be very upset with them and rightly so. Your life is more complex than a single moment.

As Pentecostals, we need to operate with a far greater degree of honor and respect. Too often, I see people looking down on those who have spent 30 or 40 years studying Scripture in its original text, copying it for us and preserving it, while we form our own opinions and so-called revelations, thinking that we know better than they do. This lack of humility is very concerning. How much can you really know when compared to someone who has spent 30 years studying the original text? Do you really think that you know better than they do?

One of my professors at my seminary graduate school was one of the translators of the Dead Sea Scrolls. I attended a school that had ancient manuscripts, but many of the professors were not spiritual believers. One of them, James Barr, was a Presbyterian evangelist with a PhD and started what is known in theology as the School of Canonical

Criticism,[181] which emphasizes that Scripture should be studied in the context of the community, not just the individual verses. Another professor, James Robinson,[182] translated the Nag Hammadi Codex[183] from Coptic to English. In the field of exegesis, my former professor edited a 53-volume commentary on the Old Testament. I do not want to argue based on ignorance, but my patience and silence sometimes leads people to think they know more than they do. Just because one remains silent does not mean that they agree with you. Often, people approach my office and attempt to explain the meaning of a text to me. I will respond by inquiring about the original text, but they are typically unable to read it. Nevertheless, they will claim to know its meaning. By the time I have finished studying the original text, they usually choose to take offense and leave. There is a reason God sends people to study; Christians must learn to honor those who work to translate and transcribe the text. There are individuals who possess more knowledge than I do, and that is part of why I respect them. They may not be filled with the Holy Spirit, but through their scholarly work, God has preserved some things for us. I cannot underscore just how important it is that we learn to honor these people.

James Robinson is one such individual. If you consult any commentary on your Bible, you will most likely find his name. He devoted over 50 years of his life to his work at Claremont, in a small office, receiving an average salary of $40,000 per year for over 50 years. Can you really compare your commitment to the Lord to someone like that? Do

---

181 Canonical criticism, sometimes called canon criticism or the canonical approach, is a way of interpreting the Bible that focuses on the text of the biblical canon itself as a finished product.

182 https://en.wikipedia.org/wiki/James_M._Robinson

183 The Nag Hammadi library (also known as the «Chenoboskion Manuscripts» and the «Gnostic Gospels» is a collection of early Christian and Gnostic texts discovered near the Upper Egyptian town of Nag Hammadi in 1945.

you think these guys are stupid just because you have been filled with the Holy Spirit? Many of these people have given their entire lives so that you may have access to the Bible. Their sacrifice makes my own seem inconsequential. Did you know very few American scholars can read Coptic? James Robinson was a member of the Christian Church. He accomplished some truly great works. Are you familiar with the Nag Hammadi Codex? James Robinson was its editor and even performed the first translation when it was discovered. Dr. John C. Trevor,[184] who took the first photograph of the Dead Sea Scrolls when they were unearthed, was also a professor at my school. I learned a great deal while attending a liberal school.

God specifically told me to go to a liberal school after I had just graduated from a Western evangelical seminary. I wanted to pursue my PhD, but God told me not to go to an evangelical or Pentecostal school. Instead, God instructed me to attend a liberal school. Coming from a Jewish background, I was initially hesitant to go. The Lord was insistent when He told me, "That is where you are going." I did not know what was in store for me at Claremont, but I followed God's guidance. It was not until I got there that I realized I would have access to ancient manuscripts.

I had planned to go to Fuller Theological Seminary. It was the Mecca of evangelical scholars and I wanted to study for a PhD in theology there. C. Peter Wagner and Donald McGravan,[185] two well-known leaders of the Church Growth Movement were there so I applied. Soon after, I received a call from a professor asking me if I had realized that I applied for a PhD program. When I said yes, he asked if I thought I could handle it. I told the man I was confident

184 https://en.wikipedia.org/wiki/John_C._Trever
185 https://en.wikipedia.org/wiki/C._Peter_Wagner
    https://en.wikipedia.org/wiki/Donald_McGavran

that I could, but then he suggested that I should do missions instead of theology, because I was in Africa. I absolutely was taken aback by his suggestion, but God had other plans for me. I asked him, "Are you telling me that because I am African, I cannot do theology and I need to do missions? I have planted more churches than you have likely ever seen. I have started denominations in Nigeria, opened new locations, and even gone deep into the mountains to plant churches." I remember asking him, "How many churches have you planted?" Eventually, the man said, "Come out and talk to the professor of theology." I was so angry!

In the meantime, Claremont, the liberal school, flew me in from Oregon to come visit the school. When I arrived, I first drove to Fuller to talk to the professor of theology. I sat in the reception area for three hours, but nobody talked to me. The professor of theology sat in his office and sent a message through his secretary saying that he would not touch my dissertation topic with a ten-foot pole. He never even saw my face and asked me to leave.

So I went over to Claremont's campus. They knew I was a conservative Christian, but they still chose to fly me in to attend the liberal school. They put me up in a hotel and took care of me. They asked me what I wanted to study, and I told them the topic of my dissertation.[186] They said, "Well, if you can do it, we're behind you."

I arrived in Claremont with my wife and two children, with less than $3,000. One pastor drove us all the way there and then went back to Oregon. I tell you this story because I believe we need to honor people, regardless of whether they are part of our immediate group or not. We need to be careful with how we talk about people. I came to Claremont as a

186 On Communitarian Divinity: An African Interpretation of the Trinity; Dr. Adonijah Ogbonnaya; ISBN 9781557787705

conservative Jewish kid, though nobody knew I was Jewish because I never told them. They kept asking me questions like, "How do you know these things?" But I would not tell them.

The professors often said, "This does not make any sense. How can you know such things? How is it that when you read Scripture, you say things that make sense?" I remember preaching in the seminary and in the chapel, and all these liberal guys were weeping and made an altar call. They were all at the altar praying with me. And my professor said, "How do you do it?" And then he asked, "How can you be so smart, and yet so conservative?" These were his words, not mine.

I still remember what Allen Moore[187] said, "I do not get you. You say you're an enigma, but I will not tell them because you do not need to get into that kind of recognition." What you need in academia is to prove your academic capacity, not your spirituality. This is what is wrong with many of our children. They want to prove to the professors how spiritual they are.

When I got to the school, a Baptist professor who was also a Baptist minister helped us evangelical kids. He told us, "Keep your 'being born again' to yourself. We do not care. All we care about is can you state your argument? We're not fighting with God; we want you to prove what you're saying is true." He said, "On Sunday, go to your church; but on Monday when you're here, talk like you do not know God and prove that there is a God. That will help you. Don't get into arguments about how spiritual you are. Bring arguments about what the text says and give us good advice. This isn't church."

He added, "It's not our job to make you spiritual. If you did not bring Jesus Christ here, you will probably live without

187 https://claremont-courier.com/obituaries/t20783-moore-33572/

him. By the time you come to seminary, you should know who you are in faith. If you do not know who you are right now, go back to your pastor and talk to him about it. Then come back later when you do know."

So I entered Claremont and immersed myself in my studies. I read everything, not just limiting myself to certain books like some evangelicals might. I read the entire hermetic library of the Western world, literally spending a month in the library reading all of it while still completing my schoolwork. I also explored spirituality, Spiritism, and occultism, among other subjects. I studied theology because I wanted to become a Christian apologist. Then, I discovered that I could access the school's manuscript center. I was fascinated as I looked at the first translations of the Bible in almost all the languages of the world. It was like being in a candy store for me. I did all of this during the semester while also studying under my professors.

I was amazed at how people would respect you if you showed them respect. Your faith may not be their faith, and your understanding of Jesus may not align with theirs, but the text always serves as the arbiter in any argument. Whenever there was a disagreement, we went back to the text. They might ask, "Why do you believe that?" I would simply reply, "Because that's what the text says."

When I heard others saying that liberalism argues that we are living in modern times and that the Bible may not be applicable in the same way. I argued, "Why not?" The first time I had an argument about homosexuality in a philosophical class, they allowed me to have these conversations. That is the difference between them and evangelical schools—you can have a different opinion as long as your argument is intact. They may disagree with your conclusion, but they look at the process by which you came to your conclusion. This was very important to me because I wanted to be an apologist. So I read Hinduism and the Bhagavad Gita, the Upanishads, the Bava Batra, and much more.[188] My goal was to be one of the greatest apologists in the world. I read Buddhist works, ancient texts I was not supposed to read, but I read them anyway because I needed to know them in order to have a conversation.

When I have conversations with Hindus, I do not quote the Bible initially. I quote the Bible at the end because they do not know it. Why would I quote the Bible to someone who does not know it? Instead, I ask them questions about their experiences and their ideals based on their beliefs, and then introduce them to the Lord Jesus Christ. I do not argue about whether Buddhism is right or wrong. I approach the conversation from a place of authenticity and the fact that their beliefs are having an impact on their lives.

I have had experiences where just by talking with Buddhists on a plane, they have given their lives to Christ without me even quoting the Bible once. After a while, they might ask, "How do you know this?" I then ask, "Have you read the Bible?" When they say no, I tell them what the Bible says. Then I ask them, "Do you want to be like God? Do you think you are God? How do you plan to achieve that?"

That is the reason why I love talking to Hindus, because they are already talking about being a god. I like to say, "Okay. How long does it take you to become a god? Maybe 10,000 reincarnations? What if I gave you a principle that would allow you to shift when you die? You just shift into your divinity; you do not need to come back that way." I never argue that they are not going to be a god. I never argue

188 https://en.wikipedia.org/wiki/Bhagavad_Gita
https://en.wikipedia.org/wiki/Upanishads
https://en.wikipedia.org/wiki/Bava_Batra

that their religion is wrong. I know it is wrong, but that is not the argument. The argument is what can my religion do that yours cannot do? I learned how to have this kind of conversation.

I started reading all the texts of other religions. I met guys who were not Pentecostals, who loved Jesus, and who were working at Claremont. They had liberal views, but they all believed that these things must be preserved. They did not translate the Bible based on their theology, which is what most Christians do. They translated the Bible based on a linguistic ruleset. That is why I use the American Standard Version most of the time.[189]

Can you guess why I read that specific translation? Because the people who translated it were occultists. I use it because I know that an occult person knows the meaning of a word. He will not change the word for anything. There is magic in the word, and to change the word is to change the power of the text. That is why I will not read translations made by evangelicals. That is why I do not read paraphrases either because they do not carry the power of the word. Although they may provide understanding, they do not address the true power of the Word of God. I want the real translation. You will never see me quoting a paraphrase translation for preaching purposes.

I read translations because I understand what it means when people claim to be translating. The translators struggle with the text and the word to find an English equivalent of the word to include in the text. Some people dislike the King James Version. The King James Version is incorrect for various reasons because the translators used later, incomplete manuscripts. The manuscripts were copies that did not contain everything. We have discovered earlier

189 https://en.wikipedia.org/wiki/American_Standard_Version

manuscripts, so keep this in mind when you criticize the people who translated the King James. They translated the Bible from the manuscript available to them. Regardless of the Illuminati being involved, they translated it with the best words they could find at the time. So before we start condemning people and acting anachronistically,[190] we must understand that hindsight is always 20/20. Do not judge people who did certain things when those things were not considered evil at the time. Remember, these men were not evil; they were scholars who translated Scripture.

It is not the same type of topic as slavery, where one might argue that it was just a practice of the time. No, slavery was a wicked thing, and those who engaged in it knew that it was wrong. You cannot justify slavery by saying that it was just a product of the times. There were people in those times who refused to have slaves. There is no way for you to justify the wickedness of slavery with Christian talk. Remember, before slavery existed in America, God delivered Israel out of slavery. God has already shown through his actions in history that slavery is wrong and it goes against His principles.

Remember, I am a Jew, so do not try to justify slavery because of a supposed error in judgment. Our slavery happened 6000 years ago. The people who read the Bible should have known, just based on God's increased interaction with Israel, that slavery is not God's ideal. It is wrong to say that slavery was okay just because it was common in their time. There were people back then who rejected slavery and fought against it. We can also point out Christians throughout history who fought against slavery. On the other hand, there were other Christians who engaged in it because their hearts were evil.

If half of the Christians say that something is wrong, you should take some time to reconsider your stance. It is not a

190 https://en.wikipedia.org/wiki/Anachronism

matter of an error in judgment, but a matter of the heart. Moreover, I have learned from liberal scholars that there are many people working in the background to translate texts for us. For example, many texts discovered in the Qumran Caves have yet to be translated. Every year, a few more are translated because it is a difficult process and is very time-consuming. Each translated book costs about $300 to $400, but many people say it is too expensive. However, the translator spent 15 years of their life translating the book! It is simply not fair to expect them to give it away free! This is a serious mistake. Instead, buy the book and make your trade count. I am telling you this because you should know what some people, who you call liberals, are doing right now. They are in school translating texts that you cannot read. Some of them keep doing that and never get married. They literally give their lives to make sure that the texts are available to the public.

It is so saddening to realize that not many Pentecostals do that. Show me one. Yet, we are the most arrogant people who think we know more because we have the Holy Spirit. Your kids do not go to university so they can do that. One thing you miss is the fact that there are hidden spiritual technologies in these manuscripts. The first people to learn about these secrets are the liberals, as they are the first ones to touch upon the Jewish mystical materials that are coming out. This is because we do not have any Pentecostal scholars to do that. These guys knew about ascension long before you started talking about it, and they have translated books upon books from ancient manuscripts about ascent and ascending.

I have watched these people, and I know many of them, even though I have issues with them being Christians. However, I am grateful to God for them. They translate these texts because they know something that we do not

know. They understand that it is necessary to combine both spirituality and science in order for Christianity to continue to be a strong and lively faith.

We talk about the Melchizedek Principle, but we forget about the harmonization of spirituality and science, which is also a part of the Melchizedek Principle. We have already covered the harmonization of our spiritual movement and about our higher consciousness with the manifestation of natural consciousness and the technological movement. Overall, the church has forgotten how interconnected the higher realm is with the lower realms.

You do not need a revival. A revival is usually an excuse for repeating terrible behaviors. Do you really want the Jonathan Edwards revival?[191] Do you want the Azusa Street revival to repeat itself?[192] You should not because if you get the same kind of revival, you will end up with the same social problems.

Pentecostalism was a Christian movement where the founder, the person God was using, had to hide his face so that white people would be comfortable not looking at him and could deal with Christ. We want to say that he did it so the glory of God would come and that he was ashamed. But really ask yourself why? Charles Fox Parham, one of the key leaders in spreading Pentecostalism,[193] did not want black people and white people to mix when God was moving. All the revivals in America, except for the Jesus movement, were race-based. The reason is simple: they were not Melchizedek movements. Pentecostalism was a pastoral revival. Think about it. It was not a "one new man" revival. We came close in Azusa Street, but in Judaism, we say that the real

191 https://en.wikipedia.org/wiki/Jonathan_Edwards_(theologian)
192 https://en.wikipedia.org/wiki/Azusa_Street_Revival
193 https://healingandrevival.com/BioCFParham.htm

transformation of the earth happens when faith and the seven sciences come together.[194]

When faith and the seven sciences come together, your faith has fully joined with the intellectual movement in creation to form a transformative technology that changes your world. However, the current state of the world is one where faith and the seven sciences do *not* come together. Your faith has not combined with the intellectual movement in creation, so your faith is only half a faith. It is a faith that often fails to manifest. You have faith, but your world is not transformed. Can you see it? Your world is not transformed mainly because you are moving in the heavenly realms. Before you start criticizing me, allow me to speak like the apostle Paul. I am moving heaven more than all of you. I know you think I am saying, "I am moving *in* heaven," but that is not what I said! I said I am *moving heaven*. Think about this. Your movement in heaven is useless if you do not have a channel through which to manifest it and transform creation. You cannot do that just by talking about it. Your speech prepares the atmosphere, but you need a vessel—an intellectual vessel—prepared to receive. You cannot change the system of medicine just by talking. You are the vessel here in this realm. Do not forget that.

---

194   https://neurotray.com/what-are-the-7-branches-of-social-science/

Chapter 7

THE FREQUENCY OF SCIENCE

The Melchizedek Principle carries with it an innate movement of intellect. It started with a sacrifice before the foundation of the world, but here on earth, it begins in your head because creation originally began in the head. The Melchizedek Principle starts in the head just as creation and redemption started in the head.

Think of it this way. Genesis 1:1-2 in Hebrew says,

"Bereshit bara Elohim et hashamayim we-et ha'aretz. We-ha'aretz hayetah tohu wa-vohu. We-choshech al-pene tehom. We-ruach Elohim merachephet al-pene hammayim." [195]

The translation is "In the beginning, Elohim..." In the Bible, Elohim is a plural word so you could also read it as, "In the beginning, created gods." But we will return to that later.

In the beginning, (Bereshit), starts with the second letter of the Hebrew alphabet, *Bet*. "Be-Reshit" in Hebrew is בְּראשִׁית. "Reshit" means "beginning." There are no vowels in ancient Hebrew so you can also read it like this: ב-ראשׁית. Instead of Bereshit, you can read it as *Be-Roshi*. This means, "from the head" or "in the head" or "inside the head." That is a long explanation to help you understand that creation comes from the head, not the heart. If you want to push it, you could also quote Paul:

Who is the image of the invisible God, the firstborn of all creation; for in him were all things created, in the heavens and upon the earth, things visible and things invisible, whether thrones or dominions or principalities or powers; all things have been created through him, and unto him; and He is before all things, and in him all things consist. And He is the head of the body, the church: who is the beginning, the firstborn from the dead; that in all things He might have the preeminence.[196]

Many Christians have created a problem for themselves by having disconnected from the head. The head is where it started. "Bet" means house. So you could read it as "Bet-

195 בְּרֵאשִׁ֖ית בָּרָ֣א אֱלֹהִ֑ים אֵ֥ת הַשָּׁמַ֖יִם וְאֵ֥ת הָאָֽרֶץ׃
וְהָאָ֗רֶץ הָיְתָ֥ה תֹ֙הוּ֙ וָבֹ֔הוּ וְחֹ֖שֶׁךְ עַל־פְּנֵ֣י תְה֑וֹם וְר֣וּחַ אֱלֹהִ֔ים מְרַחֶ֖פֶת עַל־פְּנֵ֥י הַמָּֽיִם׃

196 Colossians 1:15-18 (ASV)

Roshi" or "Inside the house of the head, God created." Or what about this one: "In the beginning: in the head He framed gods with heads."

Remember, the original intent of God was man. *You* are the original intent of God. Our problem is that we keep thinking the head is just a receptacle for gray matter and memories. The heart does not create, the head does. The head that you carry around with you is the place where God created, which means that the true functionality of the Melchizedek Principle cannot exist without an intellectual basis combined and empowered by faith. Why did Jesus have such intellectually heavy conversations with the Pharisees? Wait! Did you think Jesus was having an emotionally grounded conversation with the Pharisees? If you thought that, you were wrong. The head is the divine vessel containing the space of creation. The number of cells in your head is greater than the number in the rest of your body because of the magnetic principle that draws down from heaven.

When I went to school and started studying, I began to watch those around me. I realized that they had taken their faith and allowed their head to bring it together. In this way, they could leave something for posterity. They were willing to be drained completely so they could give you a book. I kept asking myself, "Why are these guys into science? Why does a theological and religious school have a business center? Why are they offering an MBA? Why are they analyzing the neural processes? Why do they have a section studying the neurological effect of prayer? How can graduate school plant colleges where Christian graduates are winning Nobel science prizes?" I realized they must know something we do not. I discovered that the Melchizedek Principle is present on Earth and they had touched upon it.

I know I am repeating myself here, but literally everyone I have studied in Scripture who was a Melchizedek priest was an inventor. Now you may ask, "What did Elijah invent?" Tell me, do you think he was able to part the water just because his mantle was anointed by God? Do you think, after reading about miracles like the fire that came down from heaven and consumed the stones, that Elijah did not understand scientific principles? Are you telling me that just because it involves science, it means something is not a miracle? The problem most Christians have is that they think science is not a miracle. You forget that a miracle from God only occurs four or five times in a person's life. For the most part, each specific miracle that happens in your life occurs only once, and very few miracles in your life that repeat themselves.

Before you start arguing here, please examine your thought process. Ask yourself why you believe this way.

Every miracle is a seed. When a miracle occurs, you should use your head to study what happened. If you can understand what you were doing, you should be able to create a technology to repeat the miracle in the natural world. God has given a seed of invention or a paradigm for healing to every single son in the world. But you have been taught that miracles are things that just happen and you have no earthly way to replicate it. If you treated your children the same way you treated the miracles in your life, they would never have grown up. Think about your children. They are miracles from God. What would happen if you did not do anything for them, support them, or take the time to understand how to

take care of them? I assure you, they would have died within weeks of their birth.

The reason for the lack of miraculous inventions in the church is not that God has not been giving out seeds. It is because people receive the seed emotionally. For most people, they received the seed and were satisfied, but they did not engage their heads to examine that gift; they did not put their heads to work. In the moment of miracle, they thought if they studied it, they would be walking in doubt and double mindedness.

Most people are afraid that if they look closely at a miracle as God does it for them, actually taking the time to study it to see how it is done with the intent to replicate it, that somehow they are desacralizing it. Let me free you from that fallacy. You are not desacralizing it. Remember, I said that everyone in Scripture who is a Melchizedek person invented something. Jesus did all kinds of things. I can show you what Jesus did and how He repeated things. But let us begin with Adam. The technology of making and manifesting the physical structure of animals in this world is currently called genetic science. It is not just a miracle; it is a scientific process. When Adam was naming the animals, there was science involved in maintaining the animal's genetic structure without mixing his genetic structure with theirs. Adam did not do this from the heart, nor did he allow his emotions to drive the process. Adam did it from the head. This is a very Jewish concept.

Let us move on to Enoch. According to the Book of Enoch, Enoch built flying machines. You did not really think you were the first person to talk about how Enoch was hovering with this flying machine over the watchers, did you? Tell me, where did Enoch get the machine? Every Jew knows that Enoch was a scientist.[197]

Let us consider Moses. Moses talked a lot about miracles, but most Christians seem to forget that Moses was not just a miracle worker. Moses was a king, a scientist, a geographer, and a physician. You might not know that because you have read the Bible mainly from a perspective of magic. That does not mean there were no miracles. However, for God to perform a miracle, the person must develop an intellectual capacity to handle it. There must be a suitable vessel to receive the miracle.

Now, let us talk about Bezalel. Bezalel created all the various and intricate parts of both the temple and the Ark. This master craftsman did these things from a scientific perspective, and then he imbued his creations with the Spirit so that they were able to support themselves without him touching them.

And Jehovah spake unto Moses, saying, See, I have called by name Bezalel the son of Uri, the son of Hur, of the tribe of Judah: and I have filled him with the Spirit of God, in wisdom, and in understanding, and in knowledge, and in all manner of workmanship, to devise skilful works, to work in gold, and in silver, and in brass, and in cutting of stones for setting, and in carving of wood, to work in all manner of workmanship.[198]

Imbuing his workmanship with the Spirit allowed fabric, leather, pillars, bronze, silver, and gold, to bring themselves together after Bezalel had worked on them. These items did not come from heaven. They did not just suddenly appear in the midst of the tribe. Bezalel built them. He made them and

197   1 Enoch 14:8
198   Exodus 31:1-5 (ASV)

imbued them with the spirit of Melchizedek, the Spirit that is God.

Do not forget, the Ark of the Covenant was built as a natural box. Then Moses spoke the names of God over the Ark. The Ark of the Covenant was then activated and came alive. I hope you can see there was a scientific process of intellection before any of this spiritual technology could work. This is why Jews are such great scientists. But you are brothers; you have been grafted into the same tree![199]

Let me help you with this since we are talking about Melchizedek. I do not often teach about Melchizedek. When I do, magic-oriented people think they are going to have things manifesting and falling from heaven by standing up and saying, "Manifest!" If that were the case, why exactly did God create the earth? Why did God leave all the materials in creation? Why did He create the trees? Why did He make gold, silver, titanium, tanzanite, diamonds, and all the other elements? Why would God put all this on the earth if one's simple desire to have things fall from heaven was enough?

The Spirit comes into things, but the problem most people have is that they put the Spirit first. God does not even do that. He made man as a technological principle. Man was first a fabrication of God. Yes, you are a technology! Let me put it another way. God made the technology, and then He put the Spirit in that technology to imbue it so that it could rise up, talk, and walk. In the same way, the temple was built and its parts were made. They sang over it and it came alive and stood in front of them. Moses made the Ark in the same way. He built it first, and then Moses used the 10 names

199   Romans 11:17

of God, commanding it to come alive. The Ark was imbued with life by the man of God.

When you tell Christians to learn science, they often say this is a worldly thing. But in reality, they do not understand that they *are* a life-giving spirit. But, they cannot give life if there is nothing to give life to. Since Adam died, man has been dying continuously[200] and everything he touches creates death. When man builds anything or does anything scientific, it comes tainted with death. Even though he wants to create life, man creates death. He gives you medicine that should cure your cancer, but it burns you. Man does not mean it as an evil medicine; it simply carries the residue of his death. You must stop thinking that people create these things because they are Satanists! They are really trying to help humanity, but death is inherent in their work. No matter how you mix things, there is death in whatever a person creates because the one doing it is a carrier of death himself. We need people who carry the Spirit of life to be the ones creating technology. You need *a life-giving spirit* to create things! Only then can you create a car that does not kill someone, or compound a medicine that does not cause death.

If you are not inventing, then what exactly are you doing with your life? Let me put it another way. If you are a son and you are not creating, you are allowing death to reign upon the earth. When an unbeliever with good intentions to help humanity makes clothes to help you, but those clothes cause cancer, it is because he is dead. Even the water he tries to purify kills the people he is making it for. The unbeliever does not want to kill them, but death is an integral part of who he is. Unfortunately, the life-givers are running around the world waiting for something to fall from heaven instead of learning how to create technology. Christians are sending their children to Bible school, but they are learning nothing

200   Genesis 2:17 תֹּמֹת תָּמוּת (mot – tamot)

that will ignite, expand, and vivify their capacity for creating anything. They have made nothing that they can imbue with the life they have received from heaven.

Why is it that the unbelievers and the occultists are the ones who said, "Let's go to space," and then made a machine to go into space? Why is it that you, the life-giver who comes from the realm of the heavens, are sitting down here waiting to be caught up? You believe that your spirit has traveled light years from eternity to time? If so, why are you sitting here waiting for unbelievers to break the law of light? Why are you not working to bring this technology down from heaven? You are the one who has traveled eternities and eternities to get to this place and moment in time.

If you are the one who understood and felt everything, who was present everywhere, why is the unbeliever the one who is trying to go to Mars, to the next exoplanet, and to the next galaxy? Why do you think that just moving in the Spirit is enough? Who will bring the Melchizedek Principle into real creation so that heaven and earth converge, the micro and macro come together, God and man unite, and the material realm is imbued with the power of God? If it is not you, then who will it be?

God allowed Melchizedek to observe creation before man was created, thereby embedding the Melchizedek Priesthood within human consciousness. It is part of the Christian faith to understand that creativity must be a result of faith and spirituality. Early European Christians were amazing innovators specifically because they allowed their faith to result in the creation of technology. But something has happened to Christianity where our faith is no longer

birthing technology. It is now merely consuming technology, which ultimately results in consuming death.

We need to take a step back and ask ourselves why we move in the heavenly realm and how it affects creation. Moving in the heavens and bringing knowledge to teach people is important, but to come full circle, Christians must also bring the blueprint of things back to earth. I do not mean the blueprint of your imagination like the kind of things you do in your ascension groups that does not create anything tangible. Less than one percent of those who are part of these ascension groups can take what they have seen in heaven and turn it into an architectural or technological design. Neither do they understand how to take what they have seen in heaven and create a medicine to cure people or reverse aging. What you are doing in these groups is great in that it ministers to you, but it ministers *only* to you. You speak to the atmosphere so the atmosphere is ready to receive, but where is the vessel that has been prepared to receive what the atmosphere desires to birth? Something crucial is missing in what we are doing.

Part of our problem is that we do not understand the meaning and purpose of our own priesthood. I have written quite a bit about Melchizedek, but not about what it means to be a priest. So, let us describe what a priest is. Let me ask you, is Jesus Christ a priest? Is Melchizedek a priest? Is David a priest? Obviously, the answer is yes. I am sure you will say that, as a priest, they bring sacrifices, they minister for man to God, and they are responsible for bringing God's blueprint to the earth. Those are great words, but what do they really mean?

A priest opens the dimension so that things from other realms can come to this one. A priest opens the dimensions and channels divine substance to allow and enable that which

is in the other realm to manifest in this realm. A priest opens the matrix of creation to manifest things in the realm where they stand. The priest holds the key to the matrix that opens up dimensions, allowing what is in the other realm to come to this realm. In other words, *you* hold the key. Why do you think Jesus gave you the keys to the kingdom? Your issue is that you think the kingdom is somewhere else instead of here. If you hold the key to open the manifestation of heaven on earth, the question becomes, what is heaven? Is heaven everything that is not on earth? How can that be true? The earth is in the heavens. The assumption that the earth is on earth is not biblical. The earth is not on earth; it is in the heavens.

I pose so many questions because I want you to think. There is no wrong or right answer. The process of thinking and reasoning allows you to become who you are supposed to be.

I often ask myself, what is in heaven but not on earth? You can give me all the religious answers you want, but are they correct? You say there is no sickness and disease, no problems of any kind. You say that paradise is not on earth and that the angels are in heaven. How can you say there are no angels on earth? You think about paradise existing in some ethereal place, but the kingdom of God is within you! What did Jesus mean when He said, "Today, you will be with me in paradise?"[201] What exactly is paradise? Paradise is not a place; it is a person.

I want to activate your thinking just as I do with my students. Our problem is not that we do not know things. Our problem is that we do not think that what we know is actually true. We have a tendency toward stinky thinking. We need people to force us, to push us. As long as you do not

201 Luke 23:43

get offended, your mind will begin to figure out a way. Your mind will tailor itself to find the solution.

So, why am I making a separation between earth and heaven? Many of you say constantly that you are trying to get into heaven. Essentially, what you are telling me is that heaven is not present here. By your words, you say that you are not in heaven. You are not maintaining critical accuracy in your thinking. Again, what is in heaven that you do not have here? Is everything that is in heaven present here? This is why you need a priest. I asked a very simple question. What does a priest do? Are you still going up and down, as if heaven is not available to you? What is it that God has for you that is not available to you now? What is missing on earth? The priestly consciousness is missing on earth. Christians claim to be priests, but rarely do they operate like one. You think the role of a priest only has to do with "spiritual" things? Is a guy in his lab a better priest than you? Think about what I wrote earlier. Wherever a priest is, he can bring something from another dimension into this one. A priest can take an ordinary apple and unlock the life that is within it. The priest can unlock your very cells and your DNA. The priest can use those same cells to cause other cells in your body to come alive.

This is how a priest operates. He is the person who just gave you genetic healing and used your genes to do it. You may think that because you are spiritual, you are a priest, but if you cannot do anything on earth, then what value is your priesthood?

I keep pushing believers to find a vessel they can use to train themselves. It is important to have a prepared vessel because every priest must have a vessel to capture what he brings from heaven. The first vessel is your body, but that is not enough. Let us say God downloaded something into your body. What good is it to you? What good is it to your husband if there is no way to manifest it in the concrete context where you are? What good is it to your children? Just being spiritual does not mean the divine download has any effect.

I want to challenge you. If you receive a download from God, ask God for an instrument on earth to make it real. Stop accepting spiritual downloads and holding them as if they are the end of everything. If God gives you a download, your job is to say, "Lord, I need a vessel to manifest this."

God showed me that many believers have ideas from heaven, but they are still sitting down. They think that God is just going to jump down and manifest it. Instead, they should be learning about electricity and figuring out how to bring that idea into reality. They do not want to go to school to learn how to do it. They think that God is going to descend and do it for them.

Take Moses as an example. There was not a single time when God came down and put the tabernacle together. God did not come down and put the Ark together. God did not come down and build an Ark for David. Did you know that David learned how to play music in heaven? His musical skills came from watching the heavens. The first harp David built was built after a pattern he saw in heaven. According to our rabbis, David built and created it. David put it on the head of his bed and in the middle of the night, he would imbue it with the Spirit. In the middle of the night, the harp would rise up and play itself. That is what David meant when

he said, "Awake, my heart." The harp sat on his bed and woke him up in the middle of the night.

Awake, my glory! Awake, harp and lyre! I will awaken the dawn.[202]

I want us to start thinking differently. The download of revelation is one thing, but we need more than that. People just want a revelation in this movement. Nobody is asking for a specific download. We all have revelatory downloads, but we are not manifesting anything. A specific download is an idea from heaven that has been made concrete so that it can be used on Earth. The coffee cup you drink from every morning is a download from heaven that someone requested!

Why are you only praying for a spiritual download? Can you not see spiritual technology when you look at an angel? Do you know that angels have technologies? Why do you go to heaven and come down, bringing nothing with you? Meanwhile, the unbeliever goes into the ethereal realm and then projects what they found there onto the earth. They see something in the atmosphere and bring it down. Yet, when you go to heaven, you bring nothing down.

You go to heaven to see God, which is great for you. I go to heaven for fellowship, which is great for me. But I determined that I need to understand how things function in the heavens. I need to ask God for the capacity and technology to bring that revelation down here. I am not saying you cannot manifest things through your words, but the truth is, it probably has not happened in your city. Has your city changed from all your spiritual movements? You claim to ascend to heaven, but has the murder rate in your

---

202 Psalm 57:8 (ASV)

city changed? I am not saying you are not ascending, but something is not right in your process.

Let me give you an example from my life. I have changed cities, and I can give you an example of how it works. There is a city in Nigeria where I planted the first Pentecostal church. I envisioned the city when it was still a village to become the capital of a state. Today, it is the capital of the state. The Christians from that city are reaching out to the mountains. I used to go there and visit a place where the people were naked. As a child, I preached the gospel in Jalingo[203] when the people still walked around naked. I had spiritual experiences and started speaking in order to frame the city. I wanted the city to look the way I saw it in heaven. I tried to build the church based on what I saw in heaven, but I needed an engineer. No matter how much I saw it in heaven, the building could not manifest on its own. I had to find an engineer who could also see the vision. The engineer built the church based on what he saw and it is still where they worship today. They have not changed the building. This happened back in 1979. Do you understand now? If you see it in heaven, then you have to figure out a way to manifest it here on earth.

Every single son has received a download from heaven. This is not about your theology or about you as an individual. This is about what you have seen up there. Your problem is you are only asking for spiritual things so you can preach and teach. Largely, Christians do not ask for real, concrete, transformative technology. They do not ask what the greatest need in Nashville is nor how they can use the same technology as a way of preaching the Gospel to change people's lives.

---

203   https://en.wikipedia.org/wiki/Jalingo

The church needs to start asking God these questions. We need to start asking the right questions.

Specifically regarding priesthood, we are speaking prophetically without having put a vessel in place to receive the manifestation. I am not telling you that you do not see. I am not telling you that you did not go to heaven. That is between you and God. My question is, what are you supposed to do with it on Earth? What are you supposed to do in creation?

I was in South Africa by the Cape. At that time, 80% of the people were unemployed in that city. I walked into the city and preached at the City Hall. I slept on the floor at the mayor's house. The mayor did not have any beds in his house. I stayed with a good Christian man named Derek who also did not have a bed. We went from there to preach at the City Hall. While I was preaching, everyone in City Hall looked at me. While I was preaching, I ascended into heaven and started moving things around. I saw in heaven what the blueprint of the city and the entire area was. I returned to Earth and declared, "I decree and I declare that this city will produce juice and become an economic power. It will produce juice that will be sold all over the world." Then I said, "I want a German company to come and serve as the vessel for producing the juice. I command that it be an aluminum company that comes here to tap into the city."

Notice that I did not just say, "I see a wealthy city." Notice also that I provided a vessel. I prophetically provided for the city. Nine months later, a German company moved in and established agriculture. A mining and aluminum company came four or five years later. Today, that city produces juice that is consumed throughout Africa.

A priest cannot simply talk about spiritual things. A priest must bring the spiritual things and create the vessels that will hold their manifestations in creation. That is what God did, and that means you have to have a head for that as well. We are entering the Melchizedek age, and New Agers are already figuring out that they have to speak spiritually and provide a vessel. The people who are not providing a vessel are the people who only move in the heavens and refuse to be educated. Education fuels the creation of a vessel.

You refuse to study because you want God to download, and He does, but if you do not have a vessel to capture the manifestation, what good does it do? Do you know how many believers receive downloads that never manifest? Some of you reading this might be in that situation. When you seek a download and it comes, it means God is putting work out for you. But you do not want to work because you want God to perform a magic trick. *You* are responsible for the creation of the vessel to manifest what you have seen.

Elijah said, "Bring your vessels, borrow from your neighbors, borrow not a few." [204] What happened after there were no more vessels? The oil stopped flowing. The reason your things are stuck in heaven is that you have no prepared vessel. Unrighteousness does not cause a lack of manifestation. You do not manifest because you do not have a vessel. So go find the vessels!

This is the Melchizedek Principle. The sacrifice of Christ was to create a vessel. God made man because He needed a vessel for the manifestation of His being. If God needed a vessel for manifestation, then you definitely need a vessel. It

204   2 Kings 4:1-7

is not enough for you to have a download from heaven. You need a vessel. This is why Melchizedek is such a great priest. Every biblical person that I have mentioned knew how to create a vessel. In every case, they had already prepared an educational vessel, an intellectual vessel, a psychological vessel, a structural vessel, or a political vessel. They had a vessel where the things from heaven could be held.

Chapter 8

THE FREQUENCY OF HEARING

God is not bound by time. Let me make that clear. You must understand that Moses did not participate in the resurrection. I use the term, "Garden Tomb," because that is where Jesus was buried, but it is just a metaphor for the resurrection, for transmutation, and for transformation. Jesus died at the place of the skull.[205] What does that mean? Jesus had to die in his mind first.

205 Matthew 27:33 And when they were come unto a place called Golgotha, that is to say, the place of a skull

The head, the mind, is the place of creation, but it is also the place of hindrance. You can either use this to create or to block yourself. The choice is yours. Paul referred to the natural mind and the spiritual mind, the natural mind and the sanctified mind, and the mind of the world and the mind of Christ. It describes how your mind operates. This is a very serious topic and can cause a lot of chatter in your mind.

Now the natural man receiveth not the things of the Spirit of God: for they are foolishness unto him; and he cannot know them, because they are spiritually judged. But he that is spiritual judgeth all things, and he himself is judged of no man. For who hath known the mind of the Lord, that he should instruct him? But we have the mind of Christ.[206] 1 Corinthians 2:14-16

Sometimes when I teach, I tell my students that I know they are not listening to me. I know this because they are arguing with me in their head. When they do that, their argument means they have not heard anything I have said in the past 10 minutes. When you argue in your head while still trying to listen to someone, you are causing a problem in your mind. It does not work. Most of us do not know how to listen. We listen to ourselves, and then we argue with the person outside.

The same thing happens in your marriage. Most of the fights you are having with your spouse are the arguments that you are having in your head. You are convinced in your mind that something is going on, and then you bring arguments deriving from your self-talk to pile on top of the issue. I bet that if you stopped and thought about it though, you would not even remember what the person did or said to you. Most

---

206 1 Corinthians 2:14-16 (KJV)

of these arguments are your interpretation of what they said, which means you have had a conversation with yourself.

We have all grown up with these poor listening skills. Literally everyone does it until they learn how to do otherwise. You have to stop yourself from engaging in that behavior or you will not hear more than 20% of what is said when someone is teaching. That is why the law begins with the word "Shema," which means, "hear."

The first law is to hear, not to talk. You may say, "God spoke," but God was silent for millennia uncountable before He first spoke. We really do not know just how long God was silent.

Hear therefore, O Israel, and observe to do it; that it may be well with thee, and that ye may increase mightily, as Jehovah, the God of thy fathers, hath promised unto thee, in a land flowing with milk and honey. Hear, O Israel: Jehovah our God is one Jehovah: and thou shalt love Jehovah thy God with all thy heart, and with all thy soul, and with all thy might. And these words, which I command thee this day, shall be upon thy heart.[207]

We have to learn how to hear effectively because the ear is the Aleph Principle. The Aleph א is the symbol of hearing, and it is also the first letter of the Hebrew alphabet. Your ear is even shaped exactly like the letter Aleph. The womb also has the same shape. Your ear is the place of your pregnancy. The ear is the only organ in your face that does not have protection. The ear does not have a filter, and it takes a long time for hair to even grow there. The ear is not hindered. It does not pick and choose what comes into it. The ear is the only place where you must protect yourself, with complete

---

207 Deuteronomy 6:3-6 (ASV)

intentionality, so you are not impregnated by false ideas. "Hear, O Israel."

Shema Israel Adonai Eloheinu Adonai Echad

Baruch shem kavod malchuto l'olam vaed[208]

The first law is the law of hearing because hearing impregnates you with creativity. Faith comes by hearing[209] and nothing is impossible for him who has faith. Jesus never said, "Be careful what you see." He said, "Be careful how you hear."[210] Just as the palate tests food, the ear tests sound.[211] It is important to figure out how we hear. Is your ear tuned to negativity so that you do not hear positive words? Do you only hear the things which you disagree with? Do you have one ear or many? The Bible says,

He that hath an ear, let him hear what the Spirit saith to the churches.[212]

May the Lord give us an ear to hear because we have not yet learned how to listen correctly. We listen by rote to what we have already determined in our minds, which is often the reason we do not hear when the Holy Spirit speaks. God speaks to us every day as the Bible says,[213] but what we hear is what we say to ourselves, not what God is saying. Let us work to develop the right ear.

So belief cometh of hearing, and hearing by the word of Christ. But I say, Did they not hear? Yea, verily, Their

208 שְׁמַע יִשְׂרָאֵל יְהוָה אֱלֹהֵינוּ יְהוָה | אֶחָד
https://judaism.stackexchange.com/questions/35663/what-does-baruch-shem-kvod-mal-
chuso-lolam-vaed-meen בָּרוּךְ שֵׁם כְּבוֹד מַלְכוּתוֹ לְעוֹלָם וָעֶד

209 Romans 10:17

210 Mark 4:24; Luke 8:18

211 Job 12:11

212 Revelation 2:7 (ASV)

213 Psalm 19:2

sound went out into all the earth, And their words unto the ends of the world.[214]

One of the best ways to develop an ear to hear is to read the Scriptures aloud to yourself. Hearing comes by the word of God, so just read it to yourself. The Melchizedek Priesthood is determined by God and refers to Christ. Remember, this is what the Bible says. Do you notice the passage in which the writer of Hebrews is talking about God's promise to Abraham?

> For when God made promise to Abraham, since He could swear by none greater, He swore by himself, saying, Surely blessing I will bless thee, and multiplying I will multiply thee. And thus, having patiently endured, He obtained the promise.

> For men swear by the greater: and in every dispute of theirs the oath is final for confirmation. Wherein God, being minded to show more abundantly unto the heirs of the promise the immutability of His counsel, interposed with an oath; that by two immutable things, in which it is impossible for God to lie, we may have a strong encouragement, who have fled for refuge to lay hold of the hope set before us: which we have as an anchor of the soul, a hope both sure and steadfast and entering into that which is within the veil; whither as a forerunner Jesus entered for us, having become a High Priest for ever after the order of Melchizedek.[215]

Why is the promise to Abraham tied to the priesthood of Jesus as Melchizedek? Because that was Abraham's priesthood. The same oath made to Abraham for the promise is the same

214 Romans 10:17-18 (ASV)
215 Hebrews 6:13-20 (ASV)

oath that God swore to allow Jesus to enter the priesthood of Melchizedek. God swore to it.

How many people are mentioned in this passage? In the passage, only Moses and Abraham are mentioned when the writer describes the work that is done and the servanthood in God's house. Apart from Aaron, only these two are mentioned as Melchizedek priests. The writer of Hebrews calls Aaron a shadow of the real thing.

In this passage, you see an example of the Jewish exegetical process. The last sentence summarizes the whole paragraph. The promise to Abraham is confirmed in the person of the Lord Jesus Christ. The priesthood of Christ must be tied back to the promise made to Abraham. Abraham was initiated into the Melchizedek order.[216]

Where did Melchizedek get the bread and wine, which symbolized the body of Christ, before Christ revealed it in the upper room? How did Melchizedek know to bring it to Abraham? Why didn't he bring beef jerky and soda instead? Melchizedek brought communion, and he was the first one to bring it into the earth. How could Melchizedek give communion when Jesus had not yet died on the cross? This is explained in my earlier statement about Moses and his participation in the resurrection.

You cannot simply bring something from before the foundation of the world. You must also have access to it in a historical context. That means you must bridge the two events in order to create a bridging effect. From this we understand that Melchizedek was operating from two places at once.

216   Genesis 14:17-20

Would it surprise you to know that you do not need to have communion in heaven? Why? It is because communion is a rectifying technology! In other words, God allowed for the slaying of the Lamb before the foundation of the world so that this world could be rectified. When something needs to be restored, you access the event that happened before the foundation of the world. The person who is doing it must have access to both the time before time and to the moment in its historical context. In this way, they are bridging both events so that it can function in the life of the person who is taking the communion.

Communion is both an historical event and a pre-foundational event, but one does not work without the other. Since it happened before the foundation of creation, you can use that pre-foundational event to access the historical event before it occurs. You can take an historical event like right now when you take communion after you finish studying and you can use it to access the event outside of creation, that is, before it happened in Earth's history. You can do both, which means that one event is encompassed in the other event.

When you operate from the fullness of the Melchizedek Principle, you are accessing both a pre-foundational event and an historical event at the same time. The Melchizedek priest knows how to use the historical moment to access eternity. They are the ones who can move outside of time, stand before creation, and from that point, access creation.

The timeline does not work in the same way for a Melchizedek priest as it does for someone else. History does not operate in the same linear manner for him. Jesus Christ is a priest after the order of Melchizedek. He can take human beings who are not yet born into Himself. When Jesus does that, these human beings are no longer in existence but are absorbed into Him. A Melchizedek priest is not limited by

time. However, if he should ever find that he is confined within time, the Melchizedek priest uses it as a portal and an overarching principle to access a time where there was no time, thereby altering the moment in time where he was confined. I bring up the subject of time because it is at the root of our misunderstanding. Melchizedek existed before creation and was present within creation, even though it had not yet been created. This is exactly what a believer is, is it not? Are you aware that you exist in more than one place at the same time? You are simultaneously outside of time and inside of time! Do you recall what the apostle John said about Jesus?

> **No man hath seen God at any time; the only begotten Son, who is in the bosom of the Father, he hath declared him.**[217]

That means the Lord Jesus Christ was in two places at once. He was everywhere at the same time because there is no singular form of the word "heaven" in Hebrew.[218] There are only two instances in Scripture where heaven is used as a singular noun—the Tanakh in Isaiah 63:15, and in Matthew 6:9-15 (the Lord's Prayer). In all other instances, heaven is used as a plural noun. The reason it occurs as a singular noun in those passages is that heaven is referring to God Himself. If you want to learn more about this, you can read my book *The Golden Cord* about the Lord's Prayer.[219]

The Melchizedek Principle allows you to move in a multi-dimensional and trans-dimensional manner. You have the capacity to access multi-dimensionality from within an historical moment. This may sound philosophical, but it

---

217 John 1:18 (ASV)

218 Heaven in Hebrew is Shamayim. A plural ending. The same is true for the Greek word Ouranos, which is also plural.

219 Dr. Adonijah Ogbonnaya, *The Golden Cord: The Prophetic Alchemy of the Lord's Prayer* (Venice, CA: Seraph Creative, 2009)

simply means that when you are a Melchizedek priest, you are present everywhere else in the universe. If you do not believe this, we have a serious problem. Why do you say you are seated in heavenly places? You can only do that when you operate as a Melchizedek priest. The reason you can do this is not due to your intelligence, but because God swore *twice* to make an oath. He swore by His nature and by His Word, both of which are immutable things. God cannot lie.

When I operate within the Melchizedek Priesthood, I am fully participating as a priest of God. That means I can allow things to come into this realm; I am a gatekeeper. Jesus Christ became the only begotten and took on the role of chief priest. He is the High Priest, which means Jesus took the highest priesthood. He took on the body and wore the garment of man before the fall of man. In fact, the purpose of the resurrection of the Lord Jesus Christ was to take on the body man had before the fall. This body was meant to transmute itself to the Melchizedek garment that Adam had before he lost it. All those who followed had to put on this garment before they could be transmuted. Paul talked about the body you put on as well.[220]

Where did Moses get the garment that he put on Aaron? Moses saw that garment in heaven. Aaron's garment is supposed to mimic the Melchizedek garment. Remember, the Melchizedek garment is the real thing while the garment Aaron wore was a shadow. There are two priesthoods. One is the Melchizedek Priesthood, which operates in heaven. It is the original pattern. The other one, the Aaronic Priesthood, is a shadow that operates from the earth. When Moses sees the pattern in heaven, he comes down from heaven and makes the garment for Aaron using specific threads woven

220   Romans 13:14; Galatians 3:27

in a specific pattern. And Moses said that he must do it for beauty, for majesty, and for glory.

> **And thou shalt make holy garments for Aaron thy brother, for glory and for beauty.**[221]

> **And of the blue, and purple, and scarlet, they made finely wrought garments, for ministering in the holy place, and made the holy garments for Aaron; as Jehovah commanded Moses.**[222]

Moses placed all the stones on the breastplate, which Aaron then wore. As soon as Aaron put on the garment, his body aligned with it, or the garment realigned his body, depending on the perspective. The garment was created on earth but was imbued with the same substance as the garment in heaven, thereby serving as an imitation of the Melchizedek body. Upon wearing it, Aaron became immune to death and disease. Even when Aaron engaged in idolatry by creating the golden calf, God did not take his life. And when Aaron rebelled against Moses and Miriam, causing leprosy to descend from heaven, it did not touch him. This is because the garment Aaron wore is the Melchizedek garment, though only a shadow of the true one in heaven. When God decided that Aaron should die, Moses took him up the mountain and removed the garment, allowing Aaron to pass away. Any priest who wears the Melchizedek garment is immune to death, but this is only in regards to the shadow garment.

> **And Moses stripped Aaron of his garments, and put them upon Eleazar his son; and Aaron died there on the top of the mount: and Moses and Eleazar came down from the mount.**[223]

---

221 Exodus 28:2 (ASV)
222 Exodus 39:1 (ASV)
223 Numbers 20:28 (ASV)

As long as the garment was available, the High Priests rarely died. They literally had to take it off before they could die. This priestly garment was a symbol of the garment of Melchizedek. Only a person who is redeemed, or who has been transmuted by the presence of God, can put on that garment.

Jesus came into the world and took on a human body. He was crucified, bled, and died, whether you call it going through death or not. Death is not an end; everyone will experience it. Death is a passage, not a final destination. Both believers and non-believers must pass through death, as it is a gate and not an end in itself. Regardless of whether a person dies as a believer or non-believer, they will be raised. Everyone lives forever, but not everyone has eternal life. The soul is eternal in nature, but based on your faith in Christ Jesus, it is your choice where you will spend eternity. Eternal life is the life of God, not the life of creation. This has nothing to do with Universalism, by the way.

In order to have eternal life, a person must be born from above. Unless Jesus was lying, not every member of humankind is born from above. Jesus stated that unless a person is born from above, they cannot see the kingdom, and unless they are born by water and the Spirit, they cannot enter the Kingdom.[224] This statement is not referring to water baptism, but rather to the liquid that comes from the original foundation stone. The Hebrew word for water simply means liquid.[225]

When Jesus died, He was buried and placed in the grave. While in the grave, Jesus put on the Melchizedek body because He had earned it. When Jesus emerged from the grave, there was a flash of light, indicating that He had taken on the same body that He manifested in the transfiguration. The Lord

224 John 3:3-6
225 Mayim מַיִם

Jesus Christ then had full access to that body. It belonged to Him. When He was on the mountain, that body did not yet belong to Him since He was not fully initiated until He died.

...and He was transfigured before them; and his face did shine as the sun, and his garments became white as the light.[226]

Jesus could access that body, but it was not yet His. It's like you borrowing your parent's car, but the title is not in your name. However, when Jesus resurrected, He took on the Melchizedek body, what we call the "resurrection body."[227] I have a question for you. Exactly whose body is that? According to the Bible, we are members of that body.[228] In other words, it is not Jesus' body; it is ours. Jesus is holding that body for us now because, as God, He does not need a physical body. For us who believe, the body of Melchizedek that was prepared for Jesus was made available to us.

The Lord Jesus Christ took that body into the heavenly realm, but nobody can have access to the Melchizedek body unless they believe in what Jesus has done. The body is available, and any human being can attain it, but belief is necessary. You cannot remove faith and still say that you believe. I know some of you want to abrogate Scripture.[229] But you are using sentimentality and desire for the entire world to be saved to abrogate Scripture with your Universalism. You are rejecting Scripture and replacing it with your own ideas.

---

226 Matthew 17:2 (ASV)
227   1 Corinthians 15:42
228   1 Corinthians 12:27
229   Matthew 5:17

Chapter 9

THE FREQUENCY
OF FAITH

Read John 3. There was a man of the Pharisees named Nicodemus, a ruler of the Jews. He came to Jesus by night. By the way, he did not come to Jesus by night because he was afraid and hiding from the Romans. He came to Jesus at night because that's when Jews study the Scripture. Nighttime is the right time to visit a rabbi.

We Jews are not like many Christians who refuse to work during the day because they are preaching the gospel. We work and then go home, and at night we sit together and talk. The rabbis come together and discuss the Scripture. We do this until midnight, and sometimes even all night. Nicodemus did not visit Jesus at night because he was afraid. If you read the Talmud, you will see that they often gathered at night to study the Scripture. These are simple things that you would not know if you are not Jewish.

> **Now there was a man of the Pharisees, named Nicodemus, a ruler of the Jews; this man came to Jesus at night and said to Him, "Rabbi, we know that You have come from God as a teacher; for no one can do these signs that You do unless God is with him." Jesus responded and said to him, "Truly, truly, I say to you, unless someone is born again he cannot see the kingdom of God."[230]**

Is that what Jesus says—you must be "born again?" Let me show you what the Greek says. The word used her is ‹ἄνωθεν' (anothen). The correct translation is "Except a person is *born from above.*" This is the problem with translations. Jesus says you must be born again to see the kingdom of God. That means that everyone who is born from above has a *right* to see it.

Nicodemus asked Jesus how a man could be born when he is old. Can he enter a second time into his mother's womb and be born? Nicodemus was talking about reincarnation. He was asking the question, but Jews actually believe in reincarnation. Just in case you did not know, reincarnation is an old teaching that remains in Judaism. The reincarnation principle in Judaism is different from that in Hinduism. If you try to put them in the same category, you will miss the point. When you talk about picking up someone's mantle,

230 John 3:1-3 (NASB)

what do you think you are really talking about? You are talking about reincarnation, bringing a person's anointing, and putting it in another body. It is not reincarnation like in Hinduism. Jews do not believe in that. One day I might teach on this subject and explain why Jesus could say that John the Baptist was Elijah.

Jesus answered, Verily, verily, I say unto thee, Except a man be born of water and of the Spirit, he cannot enter into the kingdom of God. That which is born of the flesh is flesh; and that which is born of the Spirit is spirit.[231]

Not everyone is born of the Spirit because not all human beings have a spirit. If you want to have an argument, we can go back to Genesis because the Bible never says Adam had a spirit. It says he was made a living soul.[232] Adam was not a spirit. Rather, he was an intellectual soul. Not one place in Scripture says Adam was made a spirit. You can impose your own ideas on that but do not say it is in the Bible. You can tell me God revealed it to you, but do not tell me it is scriptural.

Marvel not that I said unto thee, Ye must be born again. The wind bloweth where it listeth, and thou hearest the sound thereof, but canst not tell whence it cometh, and whither it goeth: so is every one that is born of the Spirit.[233]

You do not know where the wind is coming from, and you do not know where it is going. This means that the believer who is born from above does not have a location where he is coming from or going to, no place you can pinpoint, because it comes from inside of God. You cannot place God

231 John 3:5-6 (KJV)
232 Genesis 2:7 And the LORD God formed man *of* the dust of the ground, and breathed into his nostrils the breath of life; and man became a living soul (KJV).
233 John 3:7-8 (KJV)

at a specific location because He is present everywhere. So, when you are born from above, this means you were born from everywhere.

Nicodemus answered and said unto him, How can these things be? Jesus answered and said unto him, Art thou a master of Israel, and knowest not these things? Verily, verily, I say unto thee, We speak that we do know, and testify that we have seen; and ye receive not our witness. If I have told you earthly things, and ye believe not, how shall ye believe, if I tell you of heavenly things?[234]

Jesus said, "If I told you earthly things." That means that being born from above is an earthly thing. Even your spiritual birth is an earthly phenomenon because it is earth-directed. I did not say it; the Master said it. You were born in the Spirit specifically so that you can live in heaven. You were born of the Spirit so that you can come to earth and descend into creation.

And no man hath ascended up to heaven, but He that came down from heaven, even the Son of man which is in heaven. And as Moses lifted up the serpent in the wilderness, even so must the Son of man be lifted up: That whosoever believeth in him should not perish, but have eternal life.[235]

The key word here is "belief." Read carefully. The verse does not say "believe in God" but "believe in Jesus." Believing in God does not bring salvation. Nobody is saved by believing in God or the Holy Spirit. The Lord Jesus Christ is the Way, the Truth, and the Life. Jesus said, "No one comes to the Father except through me."[236] Stop disregarding what

234 John 3:9-12 (KJV)
235 John 3:13-15 (KJV)
236   John 14:6

Jesus said! There is not a single place in Scripture that says everyone shall believe. He says, "Everyone who believes," which is a conditional statement.

> **For God so loved the world, that He gave His only begotten Son, that whosoever believeth in him should not perish, but have everlasting life. For God sent not His Son into the world to condemn the world; but that the world through him might be saved.**[237]

This is a topic that many of my friends who are Universalists talk about; but the Scripture says, "whosoever believes." You cannot take that out of context. In the Greek manuscripts, all the verses are together and you cannot remove the passages you like.

> **He that believeth on him is not condemned: but he that believeth not is condemned already, because he hath not believed in the name of the only begotten Son of God.**[238]

What if God does not condemn you, but your own belief system does? Consider this. A person who does not believe in the name of the only begotten Son of God is condemned. The Scripture does not say a person is condemned because they do not believe in God. It says they are condemned because they do not believe in the name of the only begotten Son of God.[239] This means that the frequency of faith is what makes you a Melchizedek priest.

---

237 John 3:16-17 (KJV)
238 John 3:18 (KJV)
239 Acts 4:12; Philippians 2:5-11

And this is the condemnation, that light is come into the world, and men loved darkness rather than light, because their deeds were evil.[240]

This is Jesus talking in this passage, and in most translations, these verses are highlighted in red letters. This means that all the churches accept that Jesus said these words. Even the scholars who doubt who Jesus is believe that these are His words.

...For every one that doeth evil hateth the light, neither cometh to the light, lest his deeds should be reproved. But he that doeth truth cometh to the light, that his deeds may be made manifest, that they are wrought in God.[241] **John 3:20-21 (KJV)**

I like the Bible because it says, "But he who does truth comes to light." It does not say, "He who does good." If you keep reading, you will notice that even John the Baptist joins the conversation.

Your faith in the Lord Jesus Christ is what makes you a Melchizedek priest. Not everyone is a Melchizedek priest, but as a priest, you have access that others do not. Only believers have this privilege. It is incredible that we try to grant what belongs to those who believe to those who do not. This is why we say that an unbeliever has a spirit, soul, and body. The text that refers to this is not directed towards the world, but towards the church.[242] The book of Revelation you are quoting starts with, "The message of Jesus Christ to His Church." It does not say, "The message of Jesus Christ to the world."[243]

240 John 3:19 (KJV)
241 John 3:20-21 (KJV)
242 1 Thessalonians 5:23
243 Revelations 1:1

Jesus Christ is God, but not the Lord of everyone. In the context of Christianity, lordship demands submission. You cannot apply 1 Corinthians 12 to the world because what applies to the church cannot be applied to the world. When Paul speaks of the spirit, soul, and body, he is speaking to the believer and not to the world.

Christian imperialism demands that everyone must believe as you do and if they do not, you must force them to believe. If you are going to heaven, they too must come to heaven whether they like it or not. Jews do not do this because they understand something different. This is their heritage with God and you have been brought into it. Should you not listen to them, especially if they have come to understand Christ? A Messianic Jew should be able to tell you, "No, no, no, that's not how we understand it. '

Why are you creating your own ideas? I cannot find any Gentile authors in the Bible. Do you know who wrote the Scriptures? Is there any chapter or book in the Bible that was written by a Gentile? I am serious about this. Is there anyone? You say Luke? Luke was not a Gentile. He was a Jewish proselyte and a Hellenistic Jew. Do not call him a Gentile. In fact, that is why Paul could take him everywhere. There is not one chapter in the Bible written by a Gentile. So, in other words, although we have the Holy Spirit, God Himself put a specific structure in place. And from that structure, we interpret Scripture. I am not saying that you should become a Jew. However, I think you need to give them some respect. Stop acting like the New Testament belongs to you. Paul says in Romans 9 that we should provoke the Jews to jealousy, not to stupidity.

You need to understand that a Melchizedek priest is given the freedom to decide what happens within their context. I can pray for your salvation, but what I am praying for is that your will is aligned with God's. You still have your free will available to you, but if you start hurting people, God will sovereignly intervene and stop you. When Hitler started hurting Europe, God raised up America to stop him. It is all about balance. Scripture needs to be balanced, and I am saying this because I know some of you are teachers. We have to learn to balance Scripture.

I still require God's mercy as I make my choices, but that does not diminish my ability to choose. When I submit my will to God, it becomes subject to God's determinism. If you refer back to 1 Corinthians 12, it starts as follows:

> **Now concerning spiritual gifts , brethren, I would not have you ignorant. Ye know that when ye were Gentiles ye were led away unto those dumb idols, howsoever ye might led. Wherefore I make known unto you, that no man speaking in the Spirit of God saith, Jesus is anathema; and no man can say, Jesus is Lord, but in the Holy Spirit.**

> **Now there are diversities of gifts, but the same Spirit. And there are diversities of ministrations, and the same Lord. And there are diversities of workings, but the same God, who worketh all things in all. But to each one is given the manifestation of the Spirit to profit withal.**[244]

Paul uses the word "workings," which in Greek is "energematon." That means "many energies." Energies are systems of gifting that are intrinsic to your biological system, which allows you to survive. God is the Creator of the world and, as the Father of creation, provides for everyone. He will never allow anyone to be born on earth without a gift that allows them to survive.

---

244 1 Corinthians 12:1-7 (ASV)

This gifting should not be confused with a relationship with God. Some of us come with mathematical abilities, some with linguistic intelligence, some with musical intelligence, and some with the capacity to charm others with our words, but they are all gifts that God has provided. It is His gift to the world so that you can survive on earth.

Everyone on earth must eat, and God has provided so that you can eat. He does not do this because He is in a relationship with you. God would not change His nature and stop feeding you even if you curse at Him every day. Jesus talked about God letting the rain fall on the just and the unjust alike.[245] He is not talking about the water falling from the sky. Jesus is talking about a provision that God has embedded in the earth so that you can attract what you are going to eat for the day.

You are a Melchizedek priest. You are not the same as an Aaronic priest. You are not the same as a Hindu priest. Do you see just how distinct you are? That means there is a lot of work for you to do. But first, you need to accept that there is uniqueness about you that other people do not carry.

Paul says that there is one Spirit but many gifts. The Greek word used for gift is "charisma." It means to "rub something in." The Greek "charisma" comes from the same word as the Hebrew word "Mashiach." Charisma is a great Greek word for the word we also use to rub oil on somebody. When you receive the Holy Spirit, the Messianic Principle within you is reactivated. This principle is embedded in the Melchizedek Principle. The same Spirit brought forth the Melchizedek Principle in Christ, even raising Jesus from the dead. The garment of Melchizedek is woven by the Spirit of Life, and your giftings, or *charisma*, are the result of the oil of the

---

245 Matthew 5:45

Messiah rubbing onto you. This transforms your body into a transmutative device that changes everything it touches.

You are part of the hidden Melchizedek body that you carry within you. This body cannot be manifested simply through talking; it is revealed through the giftings, which serve as vessels. Helping is a vessel, and healing is a gift, but both are vessels. The Melchizedek Frequency encompasses sacrifice, sonship, kinship, rest, and faith. Faith is particularly important because *nothing is impossible for those who believe.*

About the Author

Adonijah Okechukwu Ogbonnaya (BA, MATS, MA, Ph.D.) is the founder of AACTEV8 International, an Apostolic and Kingdom Ministry that works with the Body of Christ across the globe for soul-winning, discipleship, training, and equipping the saints in Kingdom mysteries and Kingdom living. Located in Venice, California, Dr. Ogbonnaya (also known as A. Okechukwu or "Dr. O") has focused on helping believers engage the spiritual realities that have been opened up for them in the person of the Lord Jesus Christ.

He is a native of Nigeria, West Africa, and is Hebrew-born. He earned his Ph.D. in Theology and Personality and a Master's in Religion from Claremont School of Theology. He completed his M.A. in Theological Studies at Western Evangelical Seminary and his B.A. in Religion at Hillcrest Christian College in Canada. He also holds a Ph.D. in Business Publishing. Dr. Ogbonnaya is the presenter of numerous teachings found at www.aactev8.com.

Dr. Ogbonnaya is married to Pastor Benedicta and they are blessed with four wonderful children and grandchildren.

SeraphCreative

Heaven's Heart for Earth

Seraph Creative is a collective of artists, writers, theologians & illustrators who desire to see the body of Christ grow into full maturity, walking in their inheritance as Sons Of God on the Earth.

Sign up to our newsletter to know about the release of the next book in the series, as well as other exciting releases.

Visit our website :
www.seraphcreative.org

www.ingramcontent.com/pod-product-compliance
Lightning Source LLC
Chambersburg PA
CBHW051515120626
46551CB00012B/926